SYD's S
A Novel Ba

PART ONE
Wide is the Gate and Broad is the Path through Hell.

By   William Marshall

Preface.

The following novel is part fiction and part fact, it is however mainly fact, with many names and identities changed to protect those that may have been engaged in very similar events during "WW II". It revolves around the real-life story of an ordinary Northumbrian mineworker, having been taken "prisoner of war" finds himself embroiled in an extraordinary and extremely dangerous intelligence operation, setup to infiltrate "The Third Reich's" desperate plan to recruit allied soldiers from the allied POW camps of WW II. This was instigated by the Wehrmacht to create a corps of British soldiers to fight on Germany's side against the overwhelming onslaught of the Russian advance on the eastern front towards the closing stages of the war; had it been a success the propaganda gains alone for Germany would have been tremendous.

The story brings focus upon the remarkable struggle, the enduring hardships, and the often unrecognized or even acknowledged sacrifice, that the soldiers of the "Expeditionary Force" made from the early stages of the war right through to its culmination, and more so for those that sacrificed their lives and their freedom to ensure the majority of the British Army were evacuated at Dunkirk.

My thanks, respect, and admiration goes to Sydney Ryton without who's contribution, this story would have gone along with him to his grave.

Dedication

I dedicate this book to Joan so she may share the memories and stories, told me by her father, which as a rule and for the most part of his life were kept strictly to himself and were only ever disclosed to myself in the closing years of his life.

Prologue

Syd finds himself fighting a rear guarding action as a member of a machine gun unit assigned to the 51st Highland Division assigned to "The British Expeditionary Force", during the Battle of France 1940. Following the retreat from Hackenberg on the Maginot Line towards Abbeville and St Valery-en-Caux Syd is unfortunately taken Prisoner of War, when surrender of the 51st Highland Division at St Valery–en–Caux was ordered by their commanding officers to save their massacre.

The failed attempt to evacuate the 51st Highland Regiment and the capitulation of the French Army at St Valery on the 12th June 1940, resulted in Syd being taken prisoner and like thousands of others must endure a forced march taking a full month, to a site in Germany to be interned in a POW camp and it is in the POW camps towards the close of the war that the story really begins. Syd becomes embroiled in a clever intelligence plot to infiltrate the Wehrmacht's desperate campaign to recruit allied soldiers from the POW camps to fight on Germany's side and more specifically to assist them in their struggle against the overwhelming onslaught of the Russian advance towards the closing stages of the war.

Overwhelming Odds.

Chapter 1

The stark wooden bunks in the Oflag camp afforded a man little comfort, more so the ones housed in the accommodations reserved for enlisted men. The enlisted men whose sole purpose for being there was to serve and wait upon the officers interned there-in. It wasn't just the bunk; Syd was having a bad night, in fact a very bad night, fraught with anxious anticipation and perhaps a little foreboding, he'd wrestled his way through the night from one uneasy awakening to the next each time with his mind's eye and subconscious thought steering his dreams back to relive the events that had brought him to where he was that night.

Each time he awoke he wondered if he'd be able to pull it off, it was one hell of a plan and he knew in all certainty, if the Germans were even slightly suspicious and the whole thing went pear shaped then it'd be the firing squad for him and for the officer who's place he'd be taking.

It was a strange turn of events indeed that had led to Syd being interned in the Oflag with the British and Allied Officers, but there was still honor and chivalry in the German attitude towards "The British Aristocracy" and the "Officer Classes". Officer POW's were afforded the luxury of not being expected to do manual labor and as part of this privilege had interned with them some enlisted men to serve and attend to their domestic needs. Syd was one of these enlisted men and he counted himself pretty damned lucky in that respect, he'd tried the job of closely attending to the officer's needs, sweeping their rooms, getting their food from the cook house, making cups of tea, and such like but it didn't sit well with him and he'd requested, and been transferred to outside working party, gardening and so forth and this suited him much better.

The stale overpowering stench of the enlisted men's accommodations didn't help much either, sixteen men crammed into a room intended to sleep four, even so, that many men sleeping communally in the confines of a prisoner block with limited facilities for washing and personal hygiene, basically one shower per man per week made it hard to maintain personal standards, Syd; had to remind himself just how much better off he was than when he'd been in the Stalags, nevertheless he thought he'd never actually get used to it. It was early morning and as per camp regulations all lights were out and in the dark, dank, sleeping environment of the block Syd slowly lapsed back into an uneasy slumber.

As he drifted back off to sleep his thoughts flashed back to one of the worst day's fighting he'd encountered following the retreat to the Somme Valley of the 51st Highland Division in an attempt, to try and form up a secondary defensive line. The German Blitzkrieg attack had smashed through allied defenses on each end of the Maginot Line and was heading in both directions towards the center of the defensive line and towards one of the main strongholds "Ouvrage Hackenberg" in front of which the 51st had been stationed. The 51st along with three field artillery regiments (17th, 23rd, and 75th) and the 51st anti-tank regiment had been strengthened with additional territorial units and were assigned and under the command of the "French Third Army". They were still battling hard against the Nazi advance despite being cut off from the rest of the British Expeditionary Force which at this point were in the concluding process of evacuation from Dunkirk in Operation Dynamo.

Very early on the morning of the 4th June 1940 Syd along with his comrades, the Sergeant in charge of the 7-man dual machine gun battery, of which Syd was the range taker, were dug in behind a field border hedge, that lined a rough farm track. They were behind a 2-foot dry stonewalling with a hedge in front and a shallow ditch to the front of that. The hedge and wall were perfect cover for the Vickers Maxim type machine guns, and set on their tripods they were mounted just above wall height. They'd had a few hours to prepare the site and make some limited improvements to its defenses, and the two guns were set around 15 yards apart with the Vickers guns set up for cross firing and pepper potting of the far side of the field, firing through the hedge towards the direction they knew the German Army would be advancing. The field was roughly split in two by a small stream running parallel to the field track, and there was a mature wood at the other side of the field, which would afford the Germans perfect cover until the last minute however the machine guns had the slight advantage of height with the elevation of the field dropping away towards the stream and then rising again slightly towards the woods and the most likely direction the German advance would come. Command had chanced a little mounting the defenses here but figured the German's would try to push infantry through the woods while sending the panzers around on better terrain. Setting up the machine guns on a defensive position like this was an exercise they'd repeated constantly over the last 20 days or so, ever since the German push through Belgium, they'd been given a position and grid reference to set up on, to defend come what may until they were ordered to retreat to the next defensive position, in a leap-frogging type of fighting defensive retreat towards the Somme Valley. In essence, this being a rear guarding action to try and buy time for the majority of the French Third Army and the BEF, to form up a new defensive position and indeed a new defensive line they hoped they could hold south of the River Somme. At this time the majority of the BEF, had already been pushed all the way back to Dunkirk, where despite having set up a last defensive perimeter where they thought they might have some geographical advantage: That being the ground around Dunkirk was predominantly marshy and the BEF had thought the German Army would not be able to utilize their panzers to their best advantage and hoped this would buy them some time and perhaps even the opportunity of securing a fortified coastal town from which they could resupply and launch another offensive against the overwhelming German onslaught; this was not to be and left the 51st and the French army doing their best to try and stem the German advance on their own. The brutality of the German Blitzkrieg had forced the hurried evacuation of some 338,226 British and French troops across the Channel back to Britain; "Operation Dynamo" something the men of the 51st division were still unaware of or at least at Syd's level they were not.

Syd on the range finder which was set up on its tripod atop of the dry-stone wall was perhaps in the most vulnerable position of the battery, peering through the range finder which in turn was set up to look through a small clearing in the foliage of the hedge. He was in a state of heightened anticipation sweating a little in nervous expectation as he knew his success at directing the guns to effectively take out as many German soldiers as was possible could mean the difference between life and death for him as well as his small band of comrades and indeed to the majority of the BEF and 51st scrambling to set up offensive positions behind them towards Abbeville. He constantly swapped between his field glasses, and looking through the range finder, continuously checking his ranges and relaying them to his sergeant, who'd ordered that once the Germans showed, he wanted constant range updates as they advanced towards the stream and if they got across and made their way up the hill. This so the effectiveness, range, and ground fall of the machine guns could be calculated, and adjusted to maximize the kill rate as the Germans advanced.

It was still very early morning and they'd been aware of ongoing Stuka attacks happening on both their flanks for over an hour or so, but quite some distance off when they were suddenly alerted to the unmistakable sound of dive bomber attacks growing much closer to their position, so they readied themselves for yet another attack from the Luftwaffe. It didn't take long and in a matter of minutes the aircraft had closed in, identified their targets and had commenced their attack, with the unique and terrifying scream of diving Junkers JU 87's making them all momentarily look up before diving for the limited cover of the dry-stone wall, then scrambling to return small arms fire from their rifles in the vane hope of getting a lucky shot at the three diving aircraft. That is all except Syd who knew he must remain on station peering down the field to alert the crew as soon as German Infantry emerged from the forest, which probably wouldn't be long if the attack of the aircraft was anything to go by. "Don't worry" shouted the Sergeant "they're only trying to soften us up, remain focused and let's see if we can't bring one of those bastards down". Sergeant James Blackshaw known as Jimmy was doing his utmost to keep the men's morale together and he'd hardly finished yelling the advice as again the sound of a diving aircraft had them swinging their heads round to see one of the Stuka's escort fighters, probably a Messerschmitt ME 109 diving and lining itself up for a strafing attack, this probably as a consequence of there being no allied aircraft in the sky at that time to counter the German planes. Then came the first of the explosions as the dive-bomber's screaming sirens changed pitch, as they pulled out of their dives and the bombs exploded hitting or hopefully missing their intended target. A terrifying and quite deafening prattle of explosions rang out, followed very shortly by a second and then a third all a little way off but nonetheless coupled with the horrendous sound of the terror dive sirens, terrifying indeed and all too close for comfort. The sound of the first bombs was just ebbing away as the chatter of machine guns rang out and the field track behind where they were, erupted with advancing machine gun fire smashing through the foliage and branches of the hedge line behind them, but fortunately a little off target. It was again as it had been time and time again over the last few days, as if all at once they'd descended into the very pits of hell with the entire front erupting into anti-aircraft fire. Syd was a little relieved that the defensive line was pretty well spread out so the planes probably had what they thought were better targets than them. He was however a little worried that their three vehicles, carrier trucks although heavily camouflaged parked in a dip on the rough field track a little way up the track behind them was probably what was stirring interest from the Luftwaffe. Syd was still intently peering through the field glasses and trying to distance himself a little from the utter firestorm that had erupted all around them when he spotted the first wave of unmistakable German Infantry exiting the forest and advancing at speed across the field and towards the stream. Syd instinctively shouted out "Here we go again Sergeant, the beggars are out of the forest and coming towards us, and right in our field of fire". "Sergeant Blackshaw barked out the command for the men to take their firing positions and it was literally seconds before the first bursts of machine gun fire was making ground fall right amongst the advancing German Infantry. Syd still peering through the glasses could see the looks of terror and panic on the faces of the soldiers as the hail of machine gun bullets cut swathes through the advancing men, Syd gritted his teeth in horror and being a religious man knew the look on the faces of those dying men would haunt him until the day he died yet he remained on station, swapping his attention back to the range finder to take new ranges to the edge of the woods as the surprised German Infantry hurriedly retreated back to the cover of the woods.

The range finder was a Barr and Stroud optical coincidence instrument, precise and ideal at realizing ranges, but being about a yard long was very unwieldy, and required the operator to peer into eyepieces set in the center of the instrument body and needing to be presented with the length perpendicular to the target. This meant the operator was in an extremely exposed and vulnerable position to get clear line of sight to the intended target. Syd took at least four marks and was just shouting out the last to Sergeant Blackshaw when he was startled by a Zing in his right ear and knew instinctively that a bullet probably fired by a German marksman in the woods had just narrowly missed him probably by less than an inch. He ducked to take cover a little, saying to the Sergeant "Just had a bullet zinging past my right ear Sergeant think Fritz has our position".

"Don't worry" replied the Sergeant "It's the one you don't hear that will kill you," and he laughed a little probably to make a little less of just how close Syd had come to catching a German bullet. "Keep your head down a while, and let's see if we can't get em pinned down for a time," and referring to the ranging tables and from Syd's latest range marks Sergeant Blackshaw hurriedly gave instructions to re-sight and set ranges on the machine guns. In double quick time, the guns were chattering away peppering the woods, with a hail storm of lead, but unfortunately with an ever-diminishing supply of ammunition, as the driver mechanics ran back and forth from the carrier vehicles to the gun positions with fresh ammunition boxes.

"Right-Oh back on your station lance Corporal" commanded the Sergeant. "Keep your eyes peeled, we'll give em periodic bursts, let's hope they've sent the damned panzers around the woods and they're not on their way through."

Syd cautiously returned to his field glasses, this time lowering his scanning position, just an inch or two, which although leaving him still in a very exposed position gave him a little more comfort and reassurance. He swapped back to the rangefinder, and started re-checking his marks to the woods and again he swapped between the range finder and the field glasses, scanning the wooded tree line for movement, and then going back to the rangefinder; as he did so, and focusing the powerful field binoculars it was like looking into a theatre of horror. He shuddered again as he cast an eye on the dozens of bodies now littering the front of the woods some way up the field. The machine guns had stopped now, finishing their burst, or perhaps it was just that Syd was in such a high state of anxiety that things seemed to go quiet for a while, and back on the range finder he panned the powerful instrument over the dead German corpses and as he did he cringed a little with a feeling of remorse. The sight was made all the more eerie, macabre, and horrific by the horizontal split of the image he saw looking through the range finder, with the top half of the image mirrored and inverted to that at the bottom. This unique and mirroring feature of the image produced by the instrument made the grim bodies look all the worse, and more numerous than they were and even more contorted in the sudden positions where they had fell and met their violent end. Every glance seemed to etch a horrific picture onto his subconscious memory, with each ghastly scene seeming to paint a more horrific picture than the one that had preceded it.

Syd was snapped out of his momentary feeling of despondency as he became aware of the approaching sound of a motorcycle. Quite a feat of hearing, bearing in mind the confusion of sound in the front-line theater of a modern mechanized war; he turned saw the approaching bike and shouted out "Dispatch Rider." As the sound of the air attack diminished, and with the Jerry planes most probably off to land and re-arm everyone's attention was drawn to Syd's announcement and of the approaching dispatch rider. Communications had virtually collapsed within the French Army with most of their communications relying on telephone wires that had been severed or just simply weren't working. The 51st despite having radios in some vehicles was relying more and more on runners, and dispatch riders to pass on orders to the front line which in some cases were little more than verbal directives to retreat to the next defensive position. The dispatch rider finally arrived struggling to control the bike along the heavily rutted, and undulating surface of the farm track; he pulled up his machine just behind the first machine gun position and Sergeant Blackshaw keeping his head well down approached the rider as the fresh-faced youngster, "who looked as if he should have still been at school" blurted out in a breathless unpunctuated garble. "Pull back lads the order is to pull back, Gerry has broken through with panzers to the north and south and you're in danger of being flanked and cut off. Fall back towards Abbeville and you'll get your next positions on route, best of luck and watch out for the Stukas" and with that he revved up his machine and was off to the next groups, a mortar battery dug in some way further down the track.

Everyone waited, to hear Sergeant Blackshaw's response, which didn't take long, "Right lads number one-gun de-rig and get it loaded into the truck as fast as you like, number two gun keep on firing with peppering action on those woods and as soon as number one is loaded then everyone except Syd and me de-rig number two and load that into its truck also. Me and Syd will give covering fire with the Bren gun and rifle until you are on the move, then we'll follow on in Joan as soon as we can, everyone clear?" To which the whole body of men more or less replied at the same time "Yes Sergeant" and the lads started to carry out his orders in a well-disciplined but extremely hurried manner.

The unit had three trucks, two Morris 15cwt trucks one for each Vickers gun, it's accessories and ammunition boxes and a Morris 8cwt truck which had an improvised Bren gun anti-aircraft mount and carried the range finder, accessories, spares, the Bren gun, it's magazines, and additional ammunition boxes and most importantly Syd and the Sergeant. This was not the typical vehicle and equipment standard normally found in the regular army units but being in a territorial regiment "The Northumberland Fusiliers" as they were, it was indeed what they had; some of it even acquired and improvised since arriving in France. The 8cwt truck like most of the trucks had a female name painted on the bonnet, and this truck was affectionately known as Joan and as the Sergeant detailed the drivers of the two 15cwt trucks on what route to take Syd hoped and better hoped that Joan like all the times before would not let them down.

The plan swung straight into action and as the first gun was dismounted Syd took his place back at the range finder atop of the dry-stone wall, this time with the Sergeant right by his side with the Bren gun also resting on its two leg stand atop of the wall. Number two gun kept chattering away for a while but all too soon it's reassuring chatter ceased and both Syd and the Sergeant knew only too well the German's would know exactly what was going on and they'd be out of the woods and advancing in their direction all too soon. They were right; it didn't take but a minute or two after the second gun stopped firing that the first wave of German Infantry started advancing at a full running pace up the field. Syd got a clear view of it through the field glasses and alerted the Sergeant. "Right let's see just how many we can get! Syd join in with your rifle just as soon as you like". With that the Sergeant started firing short bursts down the field and Syd watched through the field glasses as one or two mortar rounds exploded in the vicinity also. The German advance slowed as some threw themselves flat to the ground while others continued on at full pace diving and jumping into the stream depression to get cover. Syd knew that there would be a hail of return fire coming their way in a very short time as the Germans established themselves behind the stream bank affording themselves excellent cover, so he took the opportunity to, disassemble the rangefinder from its tripod and stow it in its case, ready for a quick getaway; taking up his rifle at the same time screaming "I agree Sergeant let's see how many we can get" knowing all too well the Sergeant's and his own life would depend on them being able to keep the German advance pinned down long enough for all three trucks to get away. He prayed and again better prayed in his mind that Joan would not let them down when they needed her most, and that other units up and down the line, "artillery, mortars, as well as infantry" would be able to hold their own against and make their get away from the inevitable German advance. All in all, Syd knew in his heart of hearts that he'd be lucky, indeed extremely lucky to see this day or even the next hour through. In between Bren gun bursts Syd was getting off some well-aimed shots with his Lee-Enfield .303 there was nonetheless an ever increasing confidence amongst the German Infantry and as expected a hail storm of small arms fire was now ripping through the trees and hedge row on both sides of their position, fortunately the Germans didn't have a definite line of sight and pinpoint on their position and even the trucks were hidden behind the hedge and in the dip of the track so the fire was random but never the less heavy.

Luckily for Syd the lads had the Vickers guns dismounted and stowed in the trucks in double quick time; it was something they were well practiced at and the urgency of war had their procedures honed to perfection. As soon as they'd started up the engines and readied the trucks Alan Bryant one of the driver mechanics signaled the Sergeant who then gave the order to load up Joan with the range finder and remaining equipment and for the two 15cwt trucks to get going as soon as they could, with three men to a truck. Not needing to be told twice the gun crews scrambled into the trucks and they were off hightailing it northward up the track to the point where it had a tee junction, and there they turned west onto another track that crossed over the open fields and wound its way towards better hard surfaced roads and towards Abbeville.

This left Syd and Sergeant Blackwood still delivering fire down the field to hold back the advance. As the hail of German fire became all the more intense with bullets zinging past their location with ever increasing frequency, Sergeant Blackwood decided it was time for them to go, as it was clear the German Infantry were now advancing past the stream and he also realized he'd held their advance as long as he possibly could and most importantly allowed the loaded trucks to get away. "Right-Oh Syd time to get the hell out of here, when I've emptied this magazine, you take the Bren and get it mounted in the truck I'll drive and see if we can catch the lads". Syd knew exactly what was expected and as soon as the Sergeant screamed "right go" he fired off a last round in the direction of the German advance, grabbed the Bren Gun from the Sergeant, and taking both guns one in each hand ran at a stooped full speed and practically dove into the back of Joan, the Morris 8cwt truck. Sergeant Blackwood was just behind him and throwing the empty and one or two still full Bren gun magazines into the back of the truck, jumped into the driver's seat and crashed into gear the already running truck and started Northwards down the track as fast as he could drive. Syd breathed one hell of a sigh of relief as Joan sped into action, joining now what was practically an exodus of trucks, armored vehicles, field gun tractors and such like hightailing it away from the German advance. Despite being bounced around in the back he managed to mount the Bren gun in the truck mount, then loading a fresh magazine he braced himself against the canvass canopy steel frame work, and cocked the gun ready for any German pursuit. The truck's canvas canopy was folded forward with the rear half of the truck left open and with Syd standing in the back manning the Bren he found himself once again in a very exposed position, but none the less pleased to be under way, although sure that this was not the end of this day's action, but more than anything just pleased to be still alive.

Apprehension.

Chapter 2

The reality and stark confines of the prison block became all the more clear in his consciousness as Syd slowly awoke from his uneasy and troubled slumber. As he squinted to try and guess from the amount of light getting past the window blackouts, what time it was, he wondered and better wondered just how many times he'd relive in his dreams those terrible days of the fighting retreat through France; the ill but heroic fortunes of the 51st Highland Division, and more so, why and how many times he'd go over, and over, his whole life story with emphasis on his childhood every night while asleep, reliving every single second, night, after night, after night. After all none of his life had been what could be called easy, but perhaps it was more to do with the plan he was about to become embroiled in the very next day, and which was something he couldn't have even imagined would happen even in his wildest dreams and perhaps it was this that was making him think more and more about the challenging and troubled environment into which he was born, and had grown up amongst.

Syd found himself once again thinking back to those murky days, and his unhappy childhood, and he went over, again, and again in his mind the stories of how his American born mother had ended up living in a Northumbrian pit village, which was a strange situation indeed for pre "First World War" Britain where most migration was in the opposite direction.

Syd remembered the story of how his grandfather with the family name of "Lewis," so probably at some point descended from British ancestry had come to the North East of England from Pennsylvania in the USA, as an expert in mine engineering, most notably in the sinking of vertical mine shafts. There had been a great deal of resistance from the mineworkers, to the industrial development of the mines in Pennsylvania during the early and mid 1890's with the American mineworkers seeing the mechanization of their mines as replacing their jobs, so Syd's

Grandfather David Lewis had welcomed the challenge and opportunity to travel to England where his newly developed techniques of mine shaft sinking and mine mechanization were in great demand in the new coal fields being opened up in the North of England. Together with his wife and daughters David traveled to Great Britain on the recently developed Atlantic steam ship transit routes where he'd found work in England with the Broomhill Coal Company of Northumberland. Arriving in the 1890's Syd's mother Emma although born in the United States had, had quite some time growing up in the North East of England to be almost local by the time she'd reached marrying age, and she married a local man named Stephen Ryton and so opted to remain in England when her mother died in 1905 and her father and family decided to return to "The States." Syd's mother Emma had three children before the advent of the First World War; those being Hannah, David, and Stephen, and this being indeed where Syd's troubles had begun, before he was even born so to speak.

With the outbreak of war in 1914 Emma's husband volunteered to fight and although fortunate to survive right through to the final days of the war was killed three days before the cessation of hostilities on November 8th 1918 with the amnesties taking place on the 11th. Probably as a result of the shock Emma took up with another man straight away, and Syd was born on the 1st September 1919. Because of this, and to a certain extent, it had been the prejudices and narrow-mindedness of those times that had directed Syd's destiny, and molded his personality.

Even though it was blatantly obvious and impossible for Stephen Ryton to have been Syd's father, Emma being widowed and not married at that time to Syd's real father: Syd was never given his rightful name, neither was he accepted or even acknowledged as such by his real father his entire life even though Emma went on to marry Syd's real father, a man named "Edward (Ted) Morly" going on to have another three children Mary, Ethel and Daisy.

Children can be so cruel and Syd growing up had to suffer the painful indignation, callous childhood abuse, and cold-hearted profanities associated with his situation, and couldn't to that day or even as it turned out far beyond ever bring himself to use the word bastard, neither was he comfortable in the company of anyone using or associating him with it.

Over and above this Syd's real father, quite some years his mother's junior turned out to be a violent drunk, and Syd had to endure not only the physical, and mental consequences of this himself, but on many, many, occasions witness his mother being victim, and being subjected to that same level of violent abuse; something that would stay with him his entire life

As Syd lay in his bunk he mentally wrestled with these thoughts as he did every night and as always was left wondering if there was indeed anything more sinister to his whole childhood situation than that, he'd been led to believe, but as always just concluded that he would never, ever know, but realized, and to a certain extent was grateful that it was indeed this experience, "his childhood experience" that had given him the guile, strength of character, and even the courage he'd need to carry out and enact tomorrow's plan, or more so today's as it was that very morning the exchange was planned and when indeed the swap would take place.

The Plan.

Chapter 3

For some time, the officers interned within Oflag VII-B in Eichstatt Germany had been aware, in fact more than aware of the German's sinister yet more or less futile attempts to recruit British and other commonwealth nationalities from the stalag POW camps. This in an effort to form up in particular a British Fighting Unit comprised of British fighting soldiers that would be led by German officers to fight on Germany's side against what they described as the rise and spread of the Bolshevik threat. This unit to be known as "The Legion of St George" was indeed a cunning effort; basically by 1944 the Nazis were desperate and prepared to, by any means necessary recruit seasoned soldiers to help them defend Germany against the overwhelming onslaught of the Russian advance on the "Eastern Front".

To a certain extent and historically, the British Officers and men had always considered this a bit of a joke. The man who'd initially conceived the idea and took it to Adolf Hitler himself for approval; a John Amery had toured the POW camps for a couple of years distributing propaganda material in an effort to recruit POW's but had met with very limited success. The scant few recruits he'd managed to persuade to defect and collaborate, were more ridiculed than listened to during their recruiting drives but never the less the Nazi's considered it worthwhile even for propaganda purposes and had initially hoped to raise a unit of 1500 men. John Amery, a traitor and coincidentally the son of a minister in Winston Churchill's government had pretty much failed to bring the plan to fruition, and so, late in 1943, was replaced and responsibility for recruitment to the legion was turned over to the Waffen-SS

It was now late September 1944 and disturbing news had reached the officer's in the Oflag that the Waffen-SS had now elected a new German leader for the recruitment drive, and had come up with a disturbing new tactic to recruit British Soldiers into the newly named "British Free Corps". The Germans had built two of what they were referring to as holiday camps for long stay POW's one for officers named Stalag III-D/999, and one for regular soldiers called Stalag III-D/517 both at a location close to Berlin named Genshagen. The purpose of these camps was initially to transfer long term POW's there to supposedly give them a break from harsh prison camp life, however in reality the plan was to cosset the prisoners with privileges and desirable gratuities including beer and female company while at the same time exposing them to a hail of propaganda in an attempt to coerce the prisoners and convince them that joining the "British Free Corps" was indeed in their best interests. The camps had at first borne little success with the seasoned POW population quick to recognize them for what they were and they quickly became known as "Prop Camps" with many POW's refusing to go there or even once there requesting to be returned straight back to their regular POW camps.

The tactic changed however late 1944, and the Waffen-SS started to take newly captured POW's to a facility at Luckenwalde named Stalag IIIA. These POW's were mostly from the Italian and Greek theaters and once in the camp were subject to extremely harsh treatment often for days on end; in essence breaking their spirit and resolve, then after a time they'd offer the prisoners a way out of their predicament by giving them the chance to join the "British Free Corps " and using this tactic the Nazis had achieved a lot more success.

The officers in Oflag VII-B being made aware of this change in recruiting tactics and having already set up an intelligence network using homemade radio sets and by using coded messages in letters sent home were keen to get a man on the inside of the German operation so they could find out exactly what was happening and keep the intelligence services back in UK informed about what was going on, and this is where Syd had come into the plan.

It had been noticed by many in the camp, that Syd and one of the interned officers "Major John Gordon Willis" were absolute doubles in fact so similar they could have been taken for identical twins when stood together. They were both tall, being over six feet with an athletic build, blue eyes, and fair complexion and with very fair but slightly thinning hair. All in all, anyone who didn't know would have sworn they were either twins, brothers, or at the very least related in some way. The only physical difference, which was noted on Syd's papers, was a scar on his forehead, a scar he'd received in an injury working down the mines. Major Willis was of course from the opposite end of the social spectrum to Syd, being from the Scottish Highlands and having come from a very privileged background he was from a very well to do family and had come into the army through the traditional route of a military family history, public school, "Military Academy" and then into the army in a Scottish infantry regiment. Major Willis was around five years older than Syd but possibly Syd's hard life compared with perhaps an easier one led by Major Willis made them both look more or less the same age, it was indeed a staggering likeness and one the interned officers at Eichstatt were going to take full advantage of.

As normal with military intelligence operations the fewer people that actually know the better, this lessening the likelihood of any leaks, "Loose lips sink ships" being the rule of thumb so only the people that needed to know were informed of the plan. The plan was of course relayed via the internal intelligence network back to the UK and had the full approval of MI5.

The plan actually being for Syd and Major Willis to trade places, Syd would continue on in the Major's place in the Oflag so there would be no suspicions from the German side, while Major Willis with his unique and greater experience and posing as Syd would be transferred to Stalag VII-A with his mission to get himself selected and recruited by the Waffen-SS and enlisted into the "British Free Corps". The Major in preparation for the swap had slept for over a week with a woodscrew bound to his forehead and this was to replicate Syd's mining injury scar so that even the most discerning of German Guards would not be suspicious.

Major Willis was an arrogant man, very confident and above all very level headed when in action in the field. He was practically hero worshiped by the men under his command because of these attributes, and Syd for sure was going to have his work cut out impersonating him. Likewise, Syd's northern accent and working-class background may well have presented problems for the Major and in preparation each of them had spent a week or two learning everything they could of each other's backgrounds, upbringing and history, both family and military indeed everything that made the other tick.

It wasn't the first time the pair had crossed paths, Syd had bumped into; well more than bumped into the Major during the later stages of the retreat of the 51st towards Abbeville and St Valery and so had a little bit of firsthand experience of how the Major operated and his style of command; this would help Syd a lot in the coming weeks and months. The plan would be for the pair to go into the Major's room and everything that belonged to the Major would become Syd's and vice versa and that was right down to their underpants and Syd knew for sure, that from a material prospective he certainly would be getting the far better part of the deal.

Syd still lying in his rudimentary bunk-awaiting reveille found his mind cast back to that first time he'd crossed paths with Major Willis. Reveille at 05:00am would be any moment and then roll call at 06:00 so Syd thought he'd just lay awake for the short time left. His thoughts were back at the retreat of the 51st, and back to the afternoon of the 4th of June. Following their near escape from the German Infantry advance earlier on that day Syd recalled with some trepidation how the day progressed as they made good their retreat and tried to put as many miles as they could between them and the advancing German offensive. As Sergeant Blackwood drove Joan the 8cwt carrier truck closer to the main road things got more and more congested as the track became more of a high sided hedged lane, and with the myriad of French and British vehicles all funneling in towards the main road and towards Abbeville. The closer they got to the main road the more intense and frequent the Stuka attacks became, the two 15cwt trucks were still some way in front following the now heavily congested farm lane when Syd got his first sight of Major Willis who at that time was still a Lieutenant. He was in the sidecar of a motorcycle combination set up and he was being driven against the flow of the traffic with the lane just wide enough to allow vehicles to pass with great caution the Lieutenant was stopping at each vehicle as he progressed. When he got as far as Joan, Syd was pleased that they might at least get some information and idea about what was going on.

Lieutenant Willis sat in the sidecar signaled to Sergeant Blackwood to pull up and then stopping next to the driver's position proceeded to ask the Sergeant where their officer in charge was. The Sergeant quickly explained that their Lieutenant had been killed almost a week before, practically cut in two by a strafing attack and that they'd lost two of the machine gun trucks and crews also and that he had been left commanding the two-remaining machine gun carrier trucks that were some way ahead of them in the column.

"Understood" replied the Lieutenant, "Right here's what we are going to do; up ahead there is an opening to the fields on the right and there we can get across the fields where we can run parallel to the main road but off it to one side. The main road is almost totally congested with French Armor and they are trying to make a push towards Abbeville and The Somme crossings where they are making an offensive against the German bridge heads; they have priority and we need to give them as much covering fire as we can against these damned Stuka attacks. The poor sods are being bombed and shot like fish in a barrel. Sergeant I want you to turn off on the opening up ahead and get your machine guns rigged in the back of their carrier trucks. Get the tripods propped up on sand bags so we can get some elevation to fire them manually at these damned Stukas. If a Stuka dives on you then have the driver ready to get the truck moving so you are as difficult a target as possible".

"Not something we've trained for sir but we'll do our best" was the obedient reply from Sergeant Blackwood who couldn't help but think that it was almost as if he was talking to Syd dressed in an officer's uniform.

"One more thing Sergeant whatever you can salvage in the way of ammunition from the wreckage on the main road; do so, we're going to need every bullet and I mean every bullet", was the Lieutenant's parting instruction as his driver revved up and he proceeded on his way.

This was just as another swarm of Stukas was appearing on the scene and Syd was hurriedly prompted into action; still stood on the open back of the truck manning the Bren gun. Syd managed to get off a few well-aimed bursts, as the Stukas were on the turnaround having flown over the main road they'd identified their targets and were turning and gaining height for the attack. Once again, the whole scene erupted into the mayhem of war. It wasn't too long before Joan made the opening and was turning off as instructed and spread out in the field were several vehicles including their two 15cwt carrier trucks and the lads were already feverishly working to set up the Vickers guns as ordered. There were also a couple of trucks pulling anti-aircraft guns and they were making ready to fire the guns with the guns still hitched to their tow trucks. As Sergeant Blackshaw pulled up next to the two carrier trucks Syd was greeted with several comments: "Bloody Hell Syd we thought you'd been promoted" and such like, obviously the lads had noticed the striking resemblance between Syd and the Lieutenant who had just given them their new orders. Syd and Sergeant Blackshaw were soon out of the truck helping with setting up the guns in the back of their carrier trucks, feverishly placing and filling new sand/earth bags to prop the gun tripods up to give them the required elevation. The guns were set with the locking pin that held the gun to the fixed range carriage, removed, giving the gunner a much broader scope of fire, and the Sergeant as soon as the guns were set shouted out the next order. "Right lads this is the drill, let's get up there to the road which was about a mile away across several fields, park up a good distance from the road but close enough where you can fire directly at the diving Stukas and remember keep the engines running and if one chooses you as a target get the hell on the move sharpish, me and Syd will cruise the hedgerow in Joan and see if we can't scoop up some ammunition from the wreckage on the road".

With that they were off and with the driver in place and one gunner, and one ammunition feeder in the back of each carrier truck and the Sergeant and Syd in Joan in front speeding towards the main road across the fields. Nothing, absolutely nothing, could have prepared Syd for the slaughter and utter carnage he was about to witness.

Stukas just seemed to be dropping out of the skies like swarms of mosquitos as the Sergeant pulled Joan up next to an accessible gap in the hedgerow and ditch to the side of the main road. Syd and the Sergeant were soon out of the truck and clambering over the field boundary and ditch onto the road; it was truly a scene from hell that met their bewildered gaze, Syd imagined from the darkest recesses of his mind that this was what the Biblical Apocalypse would be like if indeed this was not actually it, unfolding before his very eyes. The road was full of armored vehicles, mostly French and looking up and down the road there were the obvious victims of the Stuka attacks, some having been pushed into the ditches along the side of the road and some in the process of being pushed in one way or another, some still burning filling the air with acrid smoke and with a steady convoy of slow moving vehicles trying to negotiate the battered road. There were simply bodies, body parts, and blood strewn everywhere and for a moment or two Syd could do nothing other than look on in total shock, horror, and perhaps disbelief at the scene. It wasn't for long though as the scream from another diving Stuka alerted him to the fact there would soon be bombs dropping, and possibly right where they stood. A crescendo of machine gun and rifle fire erupted from all around him with probably the lads from the two carrier trucks now contributing to the hail of lead being thrown into the air. It certainly was not this particular Stuka pilot's lucky day and a thick plume of smoke erupting from the aircraft was a sure indicator something had hit home to a vital part of the plane. The plane continued to dive emitting it's terrifying wailing siren sound, and looked for a moment or two as if it started to pull out of its dive, then something parted from the port wing and flew off and the plane flipped over and smashed into the fields on the opposite side of the road with the most deafening explosion some hundred and fifty yards away, and for a moment or two the horrendous commotion of war was muffled by the cheers of the French and British Soldiers elated by their successful but fleeting victory. The cruel realities of war had both Syd's and the Sergeant's senses heightened to the max and their mission urgency focused. Amongst the noise and confusion and running up the road passing the slow-moving vehicle convoy it didn't take long for the Sergeant and Syd to locate a BEF tracked universal carrier vehicle some way up the road with the nose buried into the ditch and the tail sticking into the air. Obviously, the victim of a strafing attack the driver's last heroic action was to steer the truck into the ditch so as not to block the road and his blood-soaked body was still there, slumped in the open driver's position at the front of the truck. There followed one of the most hectic hours in Syd's life as the Sergeant and he made repeated journeys to and from their own truck and the wreck emptying it of usable ammunition boxes.

Syd was suddenly brought out of his troubled ruminations by the sound of the 05:00 reveille call coming across the loud speakers and to some extent he was relieved that at least for another day he'd have plenty to occupy his mind and keep his thoughts away from straying back to those tortured and troubled memories; Syd gave out a little disgruntled sigh and was up out of his bunk and ready for the day.

Identity Trade.

Chapter 4

All too soon, it was nine o clock and Syd was to make his way to block III where the Major had his room, having had his breakfast if one could call it that, some cabbage soup left over from the night before, which was pretty much what they had for all their meals. Syd entered the block and preceded up the stairs and to the attic rooms where Major Willis's room was located, knocking three times a reply came back "enter" and Syd went inside and closed the door behind him.

"Right then Lance Corporal we have an hour or two, but by eleven o clock you will be Major John Gordon Willis and I will be lance Corporal Sydney Ryton, now then is there anything you think we need to go over or any questions at all before the swap"? Enquired the Major.

"No sir" replied Syd "I think I have everything pretty much memorized, I've gone over and over our shared experience south of Abbeville and all that I have told you of the retreat and surrender at St Vallery-en-Caux and I understand how best it is that the German's find out nothing of this, or at least your part in it, but realize I need to know in case any enlisted men I bump into question me on it, as for the rest, your family history, military career to date with the exception of the evacuation, your likes, dislikes, normal habits, mannerisms, I hope, well think I have everything weighed off. Perhaps just one question sir you never did tell me just how you got away from the surrender at St Valery or is it best I don't know sir"?

Major Willis went on to remind Syd that he needed to know everything associated with his military career and especially the part where he'd made his escape from St Valery-en-Caux just after the surrender of the 51st Highland Division.

"Syd if I might call you that, as it will be my name in just an hour or two, I can't stress enough how important it is you know everything about my military and private past, just in case someone, say an enlisted man that I may have served with during the Battle of France, pulls you up on it. Again, though I must stress that as far as the Germans are concerned they know nothing of my activities during that battle, or of my escape back to England following the surrender and more so nothing of the activities I was employed in from arriving back in England and up until the point I was captured in Sicily following my failed airborne operation, or putting it bluntly being dropped in the wrong spot. If Gerry were to ever find out, it could mean interrogation for you or even torture, and possibly even a firing squad. I'm not sure if you are aware Syd but Hitler did issue a directive, way after your capture, so not sure you'd know at all, that all British or Allied soldiers caught operating behind the lines that are captured are to be given no quarter, no mercy, no rights as prisoners of war and be immediately put to death by firing squad. That's because of all the mayhem that some of our newly founded regiments produced when dropped behind enemy lines; I do hope this does not put you off in any way as regards our mission here and I can't stress enough that all the knowledge you have and will have, of my past and military endeavors; keep it strictly to yourself unless you absolutely have to use some part of it to get you out of a possible situation". Syd could feel a lump developing in his throat and hoped it wasn't too obvious to The Major, but in his heart of hearts and even now knowing of this directive, Hitler's directive, he realized he'd still be happy, eager even, to get the opportunity to hit back at Gerry in any way he could. "Fine" he thought to himself "fine" but never the less, it struck all the way home and rocked the very foundation of his being, as he realized that this was one hell of an undertaking upon which he was about to embark, one hell of an undertaking indeed. Major Willis went on to explain that on that fateful day the 12th June 1940 and following the last action he'd experienced, along with the rear guard manning the south side of the box perimeter set up around St Valery-en-Caux, he'd resolutely declined to accept the order to pull back to the inner defensive ring around St Valery. He had decided escape further south was better than accepting surrender even after it was confirmed, following the initial rumors circulating amongst the French and especially when along with the order there was a notation that it was every man for himself to escape south if it was indeed possible. The Major explained that having been involved with some of the very last action where he and several infantry men had disabled a German tank, machine gunning and killing its commander as it drove into an ambush they'd prepared, with a tactically placed Vickers, then mounting the still moving tank they'd killed its occupants with a grenade thrown down through the turret hatch. Shortly after this, killing quite a number of German infantry with the last ammunition they had, then steeling the weapons from the dispatched Germans, he and the four infantrymen had escaped into the forest in the direction the German advance had arrived from. The Major explained the southern defensive line was the same defensive line as he Syd had been defending up until late that previous evening when a French unit had been ordered to take over this position, saying "remember you were ordered into the town ready for evacuation Syd so don't feel bad about it, I know you are one hell of a committed soldier". The Major went on, "We laid low Syd, hid ourselves in the forest and waited for the cover of darkness, then made our way travelling only at night time down the coast. We did bump into some Germans from time to time but luckily always either managed to evade their attention or we managed to quietly dispatch them stealing some more of their weapons and ammunition. After the first full day, we headed south then west along the coast firstly towards Le Havre, we arrived south of the town on the evening of the 13th or more so early morning on the 14th, but soon realized that there was just too much of a German offensive pushing towards the town for us to try and break through and get to the port of Le Havre. So, realizing very soon that was futile we decided to head south then west to try to get in front of the German push southward and in doing so we teamed up with some other soldiers that had freshly landed at

Cherbourg only a few weeks earlier, they'd been ordered to make their way south then west. We hitched a ride with those chaps for a day or two heading southwest during the cover of darkness and then as luck would have it we hooked up with the retreating remnants of my own regiment, some of those that had been involved in "Ark-Force", a British initiative to try and keep an escape corridor open for the retreating army, and boy was I pleased to see them. We tried to travel as much as possible, just at night amongst the thousands of retreating soldiers of all nationalities, Polish, Czechs, Canadians, and of course remnants of the 51st and more so members of my own regiment. We arrived at St Nazaire early in the morning of the 17th June to a very crowded town jam packed with thousands upon thousands of civilian refugees and military personnel all trying to flee the inevitable German advance. The roads to the harbor and docks were absolutely crammed to capacity like sardines in a tin and the Luftwaffe were having a field day as they had been for the whole retreat, bombing the retreating allied armies with their attention now focused on the town of St Nazaire and the desperate souls trying to get passage out of

France. There were officers posted to try and maintain order some Naval and some Army and being an officer myself I was afforded some privilege and my men and I were fairly quickly spirited along to the head of the queues awaiting embarkation onto small vessels, mostly fishing trawlers and such like, from where we would be ferried out to larger vessels laying off shore where they were less of a sitting target.

There; Syd I think I'll stop for a moment as I think we should get the swap, over and done with just in case something unpredicted happens to stop it taking place".

Syd had been listening intently knowing he had to retain in his memory every single scrap of information that was being unfolded and memorize it, as he knew now, his life could well depend upon it. The part where torture had been mentioned and more so a firing squad, if his true identity or even the Major's identity were ever discovered had Syd a little worried and he piped up "Sir if I might be so bold as to ask, the part where you mentioned possible torture and firing squad, I can't think of anything right now that would prompt the Germans to do that, is there more I should know?"

"Indeed, there is Syd" responded the Major, "but first let's get the swap over and done with and once we're sitting comfortably in our alternate roles I'll bring you up to speed with some of the missing parts of the jig-saw. I hadn't wanted to inform you of some information right up until the last minute, need to know, loose lips and all that, and of course there was always the possibility the big wigs would not have been happy for the operation to go ahead then you would never have needed to know".

With that the Major started to strip off, laying his uniform on his rudimentary bedside chair and he prompted Syd to start doing the same. Syd followed suit laying his tattered clothes on the Major's bed and in a moment or two both of them were standing stark naked and facing each other looking for all the world like a naked reflection of each other in a full-sized mirror.

"There you see Syd it's as I've mentioned, men are all the same in the flesh, it's education, attitude, and to some extent position, title, and possessions that set men apart, so an air of self-confidence, perhaps even an air of arrogance is something you are going to have to adopt very quickly or you'll soon be caught out. As I've explained in the past, we are two physical bodies in essence and in the flesh exactly the same but set apart by a massive social chasm and one it's almost impossible to cross. Syd I know I've said this before but I'll say it again; it would be easier for me to swindle the government out of a million pounds and get away with it than it would be for you to get away with stealing a cabbage from your neighbors garden, never forget that and keep it in mind when addressing enlisted men of the ranks, not only must you think your self above, you must be seen to be set above your subordinates and never do as I am doing now and talk to a non commissioned man as your equal. Now Syd if you'll put on my clothes I'll get dressed in yours."

Syd started to re-dress in the Major's uniform, everything from his underwear, and socks, to his uniform trousers, tunic, and shoes.

"Thanks God everything fits" thought Syd

The Major was soon also dressed in Syd's somewhat bedraggled uniform and he sort of shillyshallied for just a second or two, but soon shrugged it off then settled into the well-worn or indeed very well-worn attire and started speaking to Syd in an accent that by Syd's own opinion was a damned good impression of his own. Likewise, Syd was now adopting his much-practiced mild Scottish accent and was also carrying out his impression very well all things considered. "Good enough to fool the German's Syd, what do you think?" "I hope so" replied Syd "in fact I really hope so I believe our lives depend on it, yours on my performance and mine on yours sir".

"Right well there is no more sir from this moment on, address me simply as Ryton and I will start to address you as sir, we must do this without hesitation as if it were second nature just as it would normally be, OK sir! I'll pick up where I left off in the details of St Nazaire".

The Lancastria.

Chapter 5.

Major Willis went on to explain to Syd the series of events that had taken place on the 17th June at St Nazaire and as he started to speak while still practicing his northern accent a sullen perhaps even melancholy tone came over his voice and demeanor. Indeed, not at all like the Major but obviously the events he'd been exposed to on that fateful day had touched upon and darkened the very fabric of his soul and would probably stay with him for the rest of his life and he felt he needed to give Syd an as realistic and graphic account as was possible.

"Syd, it was carnage there is no other way to describe it and that day's events were so catastrophic the Admiralty and Government are still trying to keep a lid on it. Right from dawn and throughout the day the Luftwaffe bombing attacks were relentless, it seemed as if their dogged determination to totally obliterate everything would have no end and no mercy. As I mentioned earlier the four infantry men and around twenty soldiers from my regiment and myself had managed to leap frog the massive queues at the harbor at St Nazaire and we managed to secure a place on a French trawler that was being used to ferry French Dignitaries and soldiers out to an ocean liner laying off in the bay. As we got onto the small trawler we were crammed on like sardines and when we departed we were so overloaded I questioned in my mind the stability of the vessel but not being a nautical man assumed that the plan was to just get as many as possible off shore and onto the awaiting ships so perhaps loading limits were superseded a little, necessities of war and so forth. It was a relatively warm day and sailing out to the ocean liner would have been pleasant had it not been for the constant buzz of aircraft punctuated by the frequent thundering explosions of their bombs intermingled with the constant chatter and pounding of anti-aircraft fire. As we got close to two troop ships both ocean liners, one The Lancastria and the other The Oronsay, another air attack started and two aircraft started a bombing run, the first thundering almost right above us, we could literally feel the vibrations from the engines and plainly see the German insignia adorning the under wing and fuselage of the aircraft. Four bombs were dropped, three missing completely, sending up huge plumes of water, but one making a direct hit on the bridge of The Oronsay. We were very close approaching the vessels almost between them and the sight of the bridge on such a large vessel simply being blown to pieces was horrendous. It had been intended that the trawler we were on would deliver us to the Oronsay but being hit by a bomb clearly changed that plan of action. It was plain to see that the crew helped by the soldiers onboard had their hands pretty full trying to make good the damage and clear away the wreckage so at this point I decided to go to the bridge of the trawler to find out exactly what was going on. On the bridge, I met a British Royal Navy Lieutenant who was in charge of the vessel for the evacuation but it was being captained and crewed by its regular French crew. The bridge was being kept clear of evacuees, however as an officer I was afforded the privilege of being allowed to remain on the bridge. As the air attack subsided we laid off from the two vessels a while awaiting a decision as to what to do as there were other vessels, Royal Navy Destroyers and such like also waiting to disembark men. It took perhaps an hour and a half before it was our turn, and we were directed to go alongside the Lancastria and ordered to disembark the French civilians and troops. Seemingly the Lancastria had been ordered to sail but had declined without destroyer escort because of the distinct threat of enemy U-boat attack, with the intended escorting destroyers still busy picking up and ferrying soldiers. Once alongside the Lancastria it didn't take long to get all the people disembarked, the soldiers helping the civilians off first. There were pilot ladders rigged, the water was calm and unloading the personnel was orderly and well-disciplined with the soldiers at least, thinking they had struck it lucky to be getting such a prestigious vessel for the voyage back to Blighty. We had just about finished with the disembarkation and I was in the process of thanking the Royal Navy Lieutenant and saying my goodbyes when the air raid sirens went off indicating another imminent air raid. So, I never even got onto the lancastria, me being one of around five or so soldiers left onboard as mooring ropes were hastily cast off and we were ordered away from Lancastria. The Captain put the vessel into astern and we backed away trying to put as much distance between the Lancastria and us as was possible.

All too soon the bombing attack started with two, Junkers JU88's the first of which chose to aim it's bombing run at the Oronsay. It dropped four bombs but all missed, again landing in the water sending up huge plumes of water but doing no damage. Anti-aircraft fire had erupted from everywhere with a lot coming from Bren guns fired by soldiers on the decks of the vessels. The second bomber came in very low flying from stern to stem right along the length of the Lancastria, and it too dropped four bombs. The first bomb looked as if it had hit lancastria's funnel the second and third bombs hitting the forward holds they must have penetrated right though into the holds and with a colossal explosion, blowing the massive hatch covers clean into the air, the sight and sound were devastating to endure, and we were to learn later that the holds had been packed with soldiers, poor wretched souls probably never knew what had hit them. The fourth bomb looked as if it just narrowly missed the vessel blowing up right on the port side but probably close enough to seriously damage the hull. The explosions were absolutely horrendous being concentrated so close together and I thanked my lucky stars I was in the Army and had not chosen a career at sea. It seemed to me it was literally like shooting fish in a barrel or more so bombing fish in a barrel and I felt a certain respect and perhaps admiration upwelling inside my spirit for the courage and bravery of the men manning or more so dying on our naval vessels and that respect holds strong to this day.

The huge vessel Syd, for a moment seemed to lurch to its starboard side, but quickly heeled over in the opposite direction adopting an increasing list to port. The scenes we witnessed on deck were horrendous, some men choosing to jump straight away flinging themselves off the vessel to join the many bodies floating in the water that had been blown off the decks by the explosions. It was at this time the bombers returned on a strafing run flying the same stern to stem pattern strafing the decks, killing many more of the soldiers packed on the decks like so much cargo.

The vessel started to go down by the head and heeled right over onto her port side throwing many more off the decks into the now heavily oily water. There had been frantic attempts to get lifeboats away with only a few making it into the water and the attitude of the ship in the water now making it impossible to get any more away. It didn't seem long at all and the vessel rolled over and capsized with the propellers now sticking out of the water in clear view. Hundreds and hundreds of men had clambered onto the up turned hull probably in the hope the capsized vessel would remain afloat, obviously it was already too late for all the poor souls left trapped inside the hull.

At this point the air raid subsiding the French Skipper of the trawler decided to go back in and to try to get as many survivors as we could out of the water. Not wanting to get too close to the sinking vessel because of the danger of being drawn down with it as it sank, we stayed off about fifty yards or so. The Royal Navy Lieutenant and myself went out on deck to assist in recovering survivors; Syd it was horrendous, we tried to concentrate on those that were visibly still alive and could help themselves a little, but there were many more simply floating in the oily water obviously dead. I learned from the Royal Navy chap later that jumping while wearing the life jackets had probably broken their necks. There were also many wearing life jackets floating just below the surface of the water having jumped with all their kit on, the life jackets had not had enough buoyancy to keep them fully afloat and the poor souls had drowned with their heads just below the surface, terrible absolutely terrible. Again, we were alerted to another air attack and another wave of bombers flew in as the French Captain was getting away from the stricken vessel thinking they'd concentrate on that and the Orensay but as he did so the lancastria slowly slipped beneath the waves silencing the hundreds of men who'd been singing on the upturned hull They'd been singing "There will always be an England and Roll out the Barrel". This time as the bombers flew over they were dropping incendiaries, which had probably been meant for St Nazaire, but were being dropped on us probably in the hope of igniting all the oil now floating on the water. It was a terrible time of anticipation watching the bombs drop but then came some degree of relief when all failed with not a single device managing to ignite, the general feeling they'd been dropped too low and had not had enough time for the fuses to arm. Perhaps in their frustration the German pilots then started strafing runs, pass after pass, machine-gunning the hundreds of men in the water, it seemed relentless without mercy or compassion it was indeed an act of absolute reprehensible cowardice on their part.

As the air attack again subsided the French Captain took us back in amongst the struggling survivors and we were solidly pulling soldiers out of the water for perhaps an hour or so until the Fishing Trawler deck was absolutely packed, we would have been lucky to squeeze even just one more soul onboard. The trawler then being ordered to go alongside a Royal Navy Destroyer that had rushed to the scene all survivors transferred including myself leaving only the Royal Navy Lieutenant to return with the French crew to try and pick up more survivors. With the destroyer packed as full as she could be we set sail and arrived in Falmouth on the morning of the 19th and Syd, I was so pleased to be back in Blighty but that experience! I think it changed me as a person and from that point on made me determined to rain down the same degree of merciless terror upon the Germans in any way I could and whenever I could; and that Syd is why we are sitting here today, the thought of the Germans trying to recruit our lads to help them against the Russians and more so after the atrocities they've inflicted upon our homes, our country, and our people, they have to be stopped and stopped at any cost, at the very least our intelligence service need to know just what the hell is going on and how successful they are being so they can plan how to counter this new threat".

Syd had just sat there listening, with a lump in his throat, he'd heard of the lancastria from other internees but had no idea the event had been so disastrously catastrophic. "Seems like the failed evacuation from St Valery could have been worse had we all ended crammed into boats in that small harbor" replied Syd hoping his moral disgust at the events that had just been described, was not too evident, after all he needed to project a strong persona to get away with the mission upon which he was about to embark.

"Indeed, so Syd, and now I want you to go over it again, give me a step by step brief of exactly what happened to you following your ordered retreat into St Valery I know we've gone over this before but I want to be damned sure I have all the detail as there may be a distinct possibility I'll bump into someone that was there when I get transferred to Stalag VIIA, and I want to be sure damned sure of every last detail.

St Valery-en-Caux.

Chapter 6.

"Well Ryton" started Syd trying out his power of command and assertiveness, and doing it rather convincingly. "I'll start right from the time we were ordered to retreat from the southern box perimeter at St Valery. As you may recall we were ordered to pull back to the secondary inner position after panzer divisions broke through to the west and despite heavy fighting the lads at that end were not able to hold the German advance and as I recall that is when we parted company Major. I remember well your plan to stay behind and arrange a welcoming party for any tanks trying to get through our part of the line and would have preferred to stay there and assist on that but as you said I was ordered to retreat and before doing so we were to render the two 15 cwt trucks unserviceable. We just simply could not believe it when we were told orders from high command were to wreck everything that would be left behind and may be of use to the Germans; the two carrier trucks after all they'd sustained us through, over the last eleven weeks of fighting were more like our homes, it wasn't a welcome episode at all. We started them up after having cut through the radiator hoses with bayonets and having removed all the oil drain plugs, this we thought best as we were also given strict instruction not to set them on fire. We were also told to render the Vickers machine guns unserviceable, which as you may recall sir we did with one of the guns removing the firing mechanism, and the other along with the remaining belts of ammunition we left in your care. We withdrew to the hastily prepared secondary inner defensive ring during the afternoon of the 11th and realizing the town was now surrounded assumed we would remain there until the last units of the 51st had been evacuated. We knew things were getting bad as the artillery and air attacks on the town had not subsided the whole day amid rumors that some French Units had actually already surrendered, a lot of us thought we were being sold down the river. All we were left with was Joan the 8-cwt truck and the Bren Gun although we were pitifully low on ammunition for that, and late in the evening we were told by the officer in charge of the inner defensive barricades to make our way down into the town and the plan was probably to embark onto small vessels under the cover of darkness where upon we'd be taken further down the coast to Cherbourg or at least that was what we were led to believe at first. As we made our way downhill down a winding road towards the town the whole road was practically blocked with wrecked armor, trucks and artillery pieces. The Germans had already taken the high ground to the west and east side of the town and had moved in tanks, artillery, and mortars and the barrage on the small town had become relentless. As we were to learn later this was Major General Rommel and he'd driven his panzer units around in a southerly sweeping arc, driving a wedge through the allied forces all the way to the coast. Pretty much we thought we were done for but nonetheless no one and I repeat no one was in the mood for surrender. Arriving at the barricades on the outskirts of the town we were stopped and told that Joan too had to be made unserviceable as there was no room in the town for her and after all, we did not want to leave anything for the Germans. We were told there was no way to get any vehicles onto the small vessels that would be picking us up from the harbour, this being as the plan had changed and that Royal Navy vessels were laying offshore and onto these we'd be transferred and we were to be evacuated back to Blighty. The news met with mixed emotions with everyone absolutely elated that we were to be taken back to England but with some sadness at the thought of having to leave behind so many that we knew would now be behind enemy lines.

Sergeant Blackshaw drove Joan to one of the few places left where it might serve as part of the barricade and last line of defense against the German advance. Taking a rifle fitted with a bayonet I stabbed through the radiator, and through the radiator hoses, finally through the tyres and as the steaming hot fluid gushed forth from her cooling system like her life's blood draining away the engine ran and labored away and eventually seized and stopped amid the terrible pounding, crescendo of war; I distinctly remember I had a tear in my eye. I remember well saying to Sergeant Blackshaw, "That little truck must have saved our lives a hundred times or more, I feel like I'm murdering a friend, one thing for sure, if I ever live to survive this war and get married and have a daughter I will name her after that truck" and as I said it, amidst the smoke, noise, and confusion of the day, it felt as if I was making a pledge to destiny itself and a one I'd be admonished by fate not to pursue, and to this day that still stands, if I ever live to have a daughter she will be named Joan after that truck".

"Duly noted" interrupted the Major, "That's a very touching sentiment for a wagon, but it's little snippets like this that are worth their weight in gold Syd if I'm going to convince Gerry I'm legitimate. I know you are a religious man Syd but any little quirks or sentiments like that, you feel I should know, don't hold back I need to know your very inner self, and more so what makes you tick, please go on".

"Well Ryton" continued Syd still trying to assert his power of command, we were told by the men manning the barricade to get into the town and make our way towards the harbour as the evacuation was planned to take place mostly from there with the overspill being taken up by small boats from the beaches however, once inside the town we pretty soon came to the conclusion that our plight was a desperate one, a desperate one indeed. Amid intensive mortar fire and artillery bombardment we soon found that there was no sign of any boats at all in the harbour so all we could do was to try and find refuge from the bombardment and a bombardment that continued all through the night. Most likely or at least what we thought to be most likely, the Germans now occupying the high ground to both sides of the small tidal harbor, they were probably doing this just to keep everyone pinned down and prevent any organization being implemented for an evacuation and of course to demoralize that I'm sure was high on their agenda. The small harbour reminded me a lot of the small fishing and coal exporting harbour that served the mines and small fishing fleet back home at a place called Amble, or at least parts of it did, and being tidal like Amble it was plain to see just how difficult the evacuation was going to be. It was however easy enough to see that the Germans occupying the positions they had on the high ground were going to make any evacuation at best very costly in the way of casualties or at worst a complete disaster, never the less none of us were disheartened, comforted in thinking that the Royal Navy would more than likely come inshore in the morning and commence shelling of the German positions to the west and east of the harbour and under the cover of that fire, it would hopefully enable the evacuation to take place. Sergeant Blackshaw and the remaining lads from our unit found ourselves a well shielded spot behind some bombed out concrete and brick constructions quite close to the harbour and there along with dozens upon dozens of others we waited for first light trying to grab a little bit of rest in-between the incessant thundering reports of incoming mortar fire, sweeping bursts of machine gun fire and thunderous artillery fire although it was hard to determine the exact source of the barrage there were so many explosions it was hard, almost impossible to differentiate. All through the night the town was illuminated by the many fires burning in the destroyed buildings and then every once in a while, a building would seem to momentarily illuminate with brilliant intensity and then collapse into so much rubble with a horrendous and deafening explosion. We could do nothing other than huddle behind the limited cover and hope that we wouldn't be unlucky enough to sustain a direct mortar or artillery round or be swept by the almost constant machine gun fire from high up on the cliffs.

As the skies lightened around three in the morning it was an unexpected sight indeed that affronted our vision we just couldn't believe our misfortune as a pretty solid blanket of fog rolled in from the sea to dampen everyone's spirits. Many lads were uttering phrases like "they'll never come for us now as they'll not be able to bombard the Gerry positions", and this was countered by others saying, "yes but if we can't see them they'll not be able to see us, it'll make getting away all the easier".

What daylight did bring was the realization just how intensely desperate our plight really was, there were literally dead bodies everywhere and the once picturesque little fishing town had been reduced to little more than a collection of smoldering bombed out ruins and all the while the shelling went on and on and on, it was merciless and relentless. As the morning progressed and it was obvious no evacuation vessels were going to show up It became clear that some decisions had been made over night; groups of officers showed up all with their own particular orders and agendas, and three things started to happen as the officers went about their business. One group was going around rallying men from artillery units in the harbour area and was soon engaged in getting some barricades built from behind which some still working artillery pieces were dragged into position. Another group of officers was going around trying to identify support troops and telling them to make their way to the beaches, and hundreds of soldiers emerged from their cover and started making their way towards the beach direction, most heading east but to both sides of the harbour, all stooped and running to try and minimize the possibility of becoming a victim of a German sniper or a machine gun sweep. The third group was looking for infantry, machine gunners, mortar crews and such like and that, as it turned out was to be our fate. An infantry Lieutenant approached us recognizing our machine gunner badges and immediately dispatched some orders to Sergeant Blackshaw. I remember his words only too well especially the ones detailing the plan to buy us some more time, but more or less the words went something like this "Looks like our navy lads are stuck out there in the fog, we need to make ready to counter attack and see if we can't dislodge some of these enemy positions, right! Sergeant you and your men are to make your way back to the town perimeter or where you abandoned your guns and along the way see if you can recommission any of the disabled weapons or find ammunition even if it means liberating rounds from the dead. When this damned fog lifts wait for the bugle signal if the navy shows up you won't need to be told it'll be obvious the evacuation will go ahead and if it doesn't then we will need to fight our way out of here, we will need to at least secure a corridor out into open land. Jump to it Sergeant! Round up as much ammunition and ordinance as you can and when you hear the signal our objective will be the high ground to the south west, it's all about this damned fog let's keep our fingers crossed for the navy but be ready to fight, best of luck, spread the word, and keep your heads low lads".

After pinning our hopes all night on an evacuation in the morning these orders hit harder than a mortar round, and I'm sure I can say that without fear of contradiction, and with only the Bren gun from Joan, two full magazines for it and each man with a rifle and a pitiful amount of ammunition, we knew if we had to fight our way out, our chances of surviving the morning were pretty damned slim. Most though a very short while then quickly concluded the officer was right, it was a far better option than just being packed into a shooting gallery like so many sitting ducks and waiting on fate to deliver a mortar round or shell to the wrong spot and that was pretty much their predicament right then. A fair few others not from our small group heard the orders and decided too it was the best option and with the pitifully small amount of ammunition or equipment we had left; all quickly realized the blunder and questioned the logic of the order from high command to wreck and abandon all the equipment and vehicles, but never the less all decided they'd do the best they could with what we had left. These were all brave, brave, souls Major and we were literally trapped in a shooting gallery and being mowed down like so many blades of grass.

Sergeant Blackshaw decided to move on the orders directly and we all knew there was no point in going back to where we'd immobilized Joan as we already had the Bren gun and all the ammunition that was left. It was felt though that going back to the perimeter barricades could be worthwhile and we'd do as suggested and collect as much ordinance as we could along the way and try to get some idea of exactly how far the Germans were outside of the town. It was a long hour, a damned long hour picking our way between the piles of rubble that were once buildings, smoldering and in some cases picking amongst still burning timbers, all the while searching unfortunate soldiers for remaining ammo and scouring to find anything that would prolong our endurance when the fight started and all this amongst the German barrage that just went on, and on without interlude. We got to the outskirts of the town having spread the word of the plan to as many as we could along the way but disappointingly we didn't need to be told that French soldiers had started to surrender on mass with a great many simply abandoning their weapons, they'd started waving white flags and had simply started walking out of the town towards the German front line that we learned from the soldiers on the barricades was pitifully close to the outskirts of the town. To say that seeing the French surrendering like that was demoralizing would be as big an understatement as it is possible to make; we all knew without the French and alone we were done for, doomed to failure before we even started. All the lads on the barricades reckoned the Germans were just sitting waiting for the 51st to be bombed into submission after all why waste the men in forcing a situation where the outcome was becoming inevitable. That morning had seen an army reduced to utter despondency, as the fog lifted and was burned off by the sun it became increasingly apparent, abandoned by the French, there wasn't going to be any evacuation, not even a naval bombardment to help us fight our own way out. We simply just couldn't understand it and more and more of my fellow soldiers became resigned to their fate and believed the signal to start the offensive would come at any minute and so would start a bloody merciless onslaught with perhaps our only advantage being one of complete surprise for the Germans as they'd simply not believe there was any fight left in us, so a few took solace in that thought and we waited and waited for the signal ready and resigned to charge up that hill.

It was however we Brits that got the biggest surprise, as the German barrage slowly allayed and stopped all went quiet and we expected the onslaught of the German attack to begin at any moment, then through the silence came the haunting sound of the bugle signal echoing through the town, to our horror it was not the signal to attack it was the signal to surrender, to lay down arms, to capitulate; utter disbelief cannot describe the feeling that gripped the men, total profound and utter shock couldn't describe it, possibly there are not even the words in existence that could describe the feeling that swept through the 51st through the psyche of a demoralized army and through that town on that fateful, indeed most fateful of days".

"That's one hell of a story Syd almost as moving as my lucky escape and brush with near death on the lancastria" commented the Major "I suspect you are just as eager as I am then to get even with the Germans. Syd, there is no doubt about it we have to pull this one off and stop them in this latest treacherous tactic, oh! And well-done Syd if I hadn't have known better I would have said that was an officer giving me the account of St Valery, well done indeed Syd: you know I have a good feeling on this I think in fact I know we can make it work".

"Thank you, Ryton," replied Syd his confidence now becoming a little more established.

"How did things go following the surrender bugle then Syd?" inquired the Major still eager to soak up as much information in the next hour or so as was humanly possible.

Syd continued "Well Ryton the bugle signal hit hard, pretty damned hard, so devastating in fact that one or two decided to take their own life rather than be captured and become a prisoner of war, that was a difficult thing to watch as one soldier very close by chose to shoot himself in the head with a Luger that he must have taken from a dead German, but terrible to think that he chose that rather than face the prospect of becoming a prisoner. Our little group looked at each other with utter disbelief, even bewilderment and perhaps even disgust with each man seeming to search his soul for something from which to take solace. Sergeant Blackwood as always was the one to keep us all focused and said right away, "Right all machine gun insignia, patches badges, anything that would identify you as a machine gunner, loose it right now. We've sent so many Gerry's on their way to an untimely death they are going to have it in for us, let's not give them anything to focus their hatred upon". Everyone agreed this was a pretty good idea and if nothing else it gave the guys something to keep their minds occupied as we waited for the inevitable. Some lads being better at sewing than others; some had to cut their badges off with a bayonet or at least loosen the threads with the point of one. Once all had removed the insignia Sergeant Blackwood collected them up and walked over to a still burning pile of bombed timber and in they went. Returning he told all to simply remove the magazines and ammunition lay down their weapons and we would stand to attention with dignity next to our surrendered weapons and with our heads held high until the Germans arrived.

Lightened Spirits.

Chapter 7.

The Major was obviously moved by Syd's rendition of events at St Valery realizing that these men who'd spent the last few years in captivity had paid one hell of a price, one hell of a price indeed, but he needed to know more, much more. He wanted every detail however small; any little snippet however seemingly insignificant might help him in his mission to dupe the Germans, especially those of the Waffen SS. The Major hand on chin mused for a moment or two thinking and better thinking then came out with a peculiar question.

"Syd before you go on to tell me details of the immediate events following the surrender at St Valery, can you think of any stories from your personal life, about your family perhaps, your up-bringing or even your employment that you could say were only relevant to you, something that would convince anyone who might know a little of a northern miner's lot in life that the person they were questioning was indeed the genuine article and not an imposter".

Syd pondered for a few moments then a smile came across his face; "Well Ryton I could always tell you of my first days down the mines", to which the Major responded "Go On". "Well at the age of thirteen I thought I'd brought my career to an untimely end by an unfortunate event in the airlocks at the bottom of the mineshafts." The Major realizing, he knew almost nothing of a miner's lot responded very quickly, "pray do tell Syd I have almost no idea at all of what goes on at the bottom of a mine shaft and anything you can tell me that would convince say an interrogating soldier who may have been employed in a German mine that I am indeed the genuine article and who I say I'm going to be would be good to know.

With his mind, back down the mines Syd did momentarily slip back into his normal character and the Major immediately corrected him on it. "As if you were me Syd keep up the façade". Syd started again, this time grinning a little in anticipation of the story he was about to unfold. Syd began, "My first job down the mine at Radcliffe was to operate the airlocks at the shaft bottoms letting the ponies pulling the tubs of coal through. Pushing open one door the pony would pull its tub of coal into the lock then I had to close the doors behind it and open the ones in front so the pony could continue on its way and in doing this ventilation was maintained throughout the mine. Large fans situated in the shrouded pit head winding gear tower would pull air out of the mine and this action would draw air all the way through the mine with the draft going all the way back to the second un-shrouded pit head gear. A careless error in opening or closing the doors would stop ventilation, right through the mine albeit just for the time it took to correct the error. We had one particularly obstreperous pony that would not cooperate at all in the process and would remain in the first doorjamb stopping the doors being operated and effectively delaying the whole operation. I knew the order the ponies would present at the airlock and having had problems with this pony for some days I decided that it needed a little persuasion. To assist me in my task in the almost total darkness in the airlock all I had was a regular miners lamp, which gave off a dim glow at best, and a shovel to clean up any spillage from the tubs in the airlock that might obstruct the doors. I had decided the next time the stroppy pony stopped in the doorjamb I'd wallop it with the back or flat side of my shovel to prompt it into action and to let it know I wasn't going to be messed around. The shift went on and I counted the ponies coming through the lock so I knew it was the stroppy ponies turn next. I could hear the animal approaching by the steel on steel screech of the tub wheels on the rails, and the clip clop noise of its hooves. In the all but practical darkness of the airlock and screaming "Get by you little shit" I launched a swinging and downward blow towards where I thought the animals head and shoulders would be as it pushed open the doors and stopped as usual in the doorjamb. The shovel certainly hit home on something, it was something a little higher than where I expected the animal's shoulder to be, and as the shovel hit home with a sickening thud a loud-echoing scream rang out in the airlock and echoed away into the distance down the gate, the gate of course being the underground roadway. To my horror I realized straight away this was not the noise of a startled pony but the surprised yell of the pit deputy in obvious pain. He'd found the stroppy pony loitering further down the gate and had decided to lead the animal so it would not obstruct the ponies following it. The sudden whack dropped the deputy like a stone but fortunately he'd been wearing his hard hat so his head had received only a glancing blow with the lion's share of the blow landing on his left shoulder. To say he was angry was indeed an understatement, and shouting in rage he was soon on his feet again, kicking and punching into the darkness with one of the blows landing clean on my cheek. His name was Archie and he was a big man and one thing for sure I certainly felt the pain of his angry retort. Archie soon realized what had happened and calmed down but snarled that he'd see me above ground after my shift.

The next few hours were the most worrying of my life, I felt sure I'd be sacked and never allowed back down a mine again. The feeling of guilt was overwhelming, as I knew my mother had welcomed my employment down the mine and was depending to a certain degree on the money I would be making and I could not think of how I was going to explain to her that I'd lost my prospective income meager though it was going to be".

The Major laughed, "That's an incredible story Syd, absolutely golden, no way could you make something like that up, that's just the sort of thing I was looking for, but please continue and finish the story what happened when you got above ground as I take it you weren't sacked?"

The Major was obviously pleased that the exchange of information between the two of them had lightened a little, as it had been getting a tad morbid with the previous exchanges.

Syd also feeling his spirits lifted a little continued with a slight grin on his face pleased too that he'd managed to recall something that the Major would find useful.

"The journey up above ground was the worst more so having to wait until the last lift in the cage as being a 13-year-old boy my turn was way down in the pecking order. When I emerged from the cage the pit deputy and at least twenty of the men were waiting and I thought I was in for a good hiding, being new to the mining game I imagined this must be how mineworker's justice was dished out. The deputy approached with quite a sullen look upon his face and was closely followed by the rest of the men who'd obviously been prepped and briefed regarding the incident and I mentally readied myself for the onslaught that I was sure was about to begin". The Deputy bellowed in a very deep voice, "Right lad come here" as he grabbed me around the shoulder and I can honestly say I was absolutely petrified but my worried demeanor was soon dispelled when his initial seemingly bullying tactic turned to him shouting "Right three cheers for young Sydney, he's a gutsy young lad and obviously has what it takes to be a miner". This was followed by a rapturous "Hip-Hip Hooray, Hip-Hip Hooray, Hip-Hip Hooray, the 20 or so men obviously having been briefed on the ploy as I'd waited my turn at the bottom of the shaft. I think that was the day I actually became a man and my status amongst the community was for sure elevated after that event. Needless to say, the relief that went through my mind was overwhelming but mostly the relief that I hadn't lost my mother the addition to the family income that she'd been relying so heavily upon".

"Quite unique and amazing Syd, that's one of the funniest things I've heard in years, I had no idea there existed such camaraderie and brethren spirit in the mining industry, I imagine it must be quite like in the army, when we were fighting, with everyone dependent on everyone else knowing and doing their job and doing it well and without hesitation".

"Indeed Ryton", replied Syd " It's not just down the mine but the whole community that supports it, where everything exists to serve the best interests of the mine and its relentless pursuit to produce coal. Everything in it, everything around it, everything on it, built and produced by it, and the people and community too, absolutely everything, indeed not just an industry but a whole way of life, and a tough one at that, Ryton, but I stress a community and way of life that is all that I know and a way of life that I love".

"Commendable Syd commendable indeed" muttered The Major as he realized he knew nothing of the working-class lot in life but realized he was getting a firsthand insight into life at the other end of the scale and a life at the thin edge of the wedge.

"We must press on though Syd time is short and we have a lot to discuss, I must tell you of my exploits back in Blighty but first Syd I want you to tell me of your capture and The March. The march that I've heard so much about, and don't spare me the detail, I need to know of the horrors you endured, let's start from the bugle call that signaled the surrender, we'll start there going over some of the same ground we have already covered and hopefully fill in all the blanks between then and now.

The Bugle Call and Beyond.

Chapter 8.

Syd once more mentally prepared himself to journey back in his mind's eye to that time, the bugle call, that day of abject misery and despondency and he shuddered a little at the thought but nonetheless drawing inspiration from he knew not where, he began.

"Well Ryton, back to the bugle call and beyond; as I've mentioned to say that the bugle call sounded the start of hell would be an understatement, again as I've mentioned the surrender hit different soldiers in different ways, some descending into the pits of apathy even to the point of suicide, some just milling around in dis-array, some deciding to fend for themselves they scaled the barriers and were off to take their chances on their own against the Germans. We stood strong our little band united under the command of Sergeant Blackshaw, and even at this late stage and after having removed our machine gunner identification we still had hope that the game might yet change and swing in our direction. It seemed like an eternity that we stood there to attention next to our laid down arms, meager though they were, but conversation and supposition was rife. It may have just been Sergeant Blackshaw's way of calming the situation but he briefed everyone instructing them that the signal to attack may yet still come. That is why our weapons were just at our feet and we were ready to move at short notice. The Sergeant was convinced that the Germans would want to make a full-blooded show of the surrender and he believed wholeheartedly that once the town filled with German Officers and men then there was no way their own artillery and tanks on the high ground would open fire on the town, he also concluded that with the fog having lifted the navy would be able to start a barrage on the high ground occupied by the Germans and an opportunity for a counter attack was still on the cards. I remember his words as clearly as if it were yesterday, 'it's going to be bloody lads, damned bloody but if that signal to attack, unethical though it may be, if it comes, then get your weapons to bare on anything in a jack boot and make every damned shot count'. It was an eternity, of that there is no doubt as that is indeed how it felt, but firstly tanks rolled into the town followed by halftracks mounted with heavy caliber machine guns followed by truck after truck of German foot soldiers, all escorted in turn by infantry marching behind the vehicles, weapons at the ready, and every passing moment filled the air with an increasing feeling of anxiety and apprehension as mentally we readied ourselves for the signal to attack but alas a signal that never ever came. News of the French capitulation and of the surrender of Major General Fortune to General Major Rommel spread like wildfire serving to dash our spirits even lower and the more the town flooded with Germans the less the likelihood of that attack signal ever coming, became more and more apparent. The Germans with their efficiency and military prowess were quick to herd us into organized groups, arranged into rank and file where it was possible to do so. They seemed relatively well mannered to begin with and this we took for some sort of military respect, perhaps a reverence for a worthy but unlucky opponent, and some even offered cigarettes as we were systematically searched for weapons at gun point, but the more herded and disarmed and vulnerable or more so defenseless we became, the more this turned to supervision by jack boot and persuasion by rifle butt. Now we were seeing the true nature of our enemy, up close and personal these soldiers were arrogant and heartless and indeed this was an early indication of how our future captivity was going to be. Sporadic gun fire still rang out from time to time", and Syd grinned a little as he said it, "I now know Ryton you probably had some part in that, and we all hoped and better hoped that enough of our men would get away and there might still yet be some chance of a counter attack.

"Yes, indeed Syd, if only we had developed our airborne forces quicker than we did, things may well have been oh so different, but that's a different part of the story Syd and a part I'll fill you in on shortly" interrupted The Major.

"Go on Syd I want to know of the early period of capture and of the march and to use a pun time is marching on, so back to the story or time line."

Syd again began his rendition; "By the time it came to our turn to be searched and disarmed it was late in the day, and we'd had several hours stood there to attention awaiting our fate and contemplating how we were going to cope with the next day or two. Again, it had been Sergeant Blackshaw that had kept us focused. He'd muttered time and time again. 'Right lads stay strong, try to stick together, don't give them any excuse to single you out. They will be looking for individuals to make examples of, we may yet get the opportunity to escape and remember not a work about our specialty, machine gunners are going to be at the top of their hate list!' Those words from the Sergeant were said with such passion conviction and direction, I feel as if they are etched upon my very soul, there for all eternity and to a great degree those words are what bonded us together and kept us going over the coming days. The systematic search when it came to my turn was harsh, with our rifles and ammunition having been quickly spirited away, each soldier was searched by a trio of German soldiers and confronted with one steely eyed infantryman, I had the business end of a rifle stuck right in my face as the search and frisk down began. The infantryman firstly stared straight into my fixed gaze, I felt his intense stare penetrate right through to the very fabric of my soul and I wondered and better wondered just how many, such as he, I had dispatched to an early grave and for a while that thought made me feel better. The man was fiercely arrogant with a disturbing superior air, almost as if he was too good for such a menial task and roughly indeed very roughly I was frisked down for concealed weapons, finding nothing a third infantryman struck me on my right shoulder and chest with the butt of his rifle knocking me to the ground. I had readied myself for more of the same but the searching Nazis moved quickly down the line with not everyone but many receiving some sort of bludgeoning action which I realize now was probably not only to demoralize but also to weaken those that looked strong enough to still pose a physical threat.

We and by that, I mean our little group together with around another thirty or so were grouped together and under the barked but very poorly issued English orders we were marched out of the smoldering remains of the town towards the south, travelling uphill along the same winding road we had entered St Valery from the day before. It was damned hot by now as day light started to fade when we were halted next to a field that had been roughly prepared as a what I can only describe as a holding pen. The field was walled with dry crumbling stone walls all the way round with rough scrub hedging behind and at the corners of the field vehicles fitted with mounted machine guns were stations and a tank was at the entrance to the field. We were marched into the field and along with hundreds upon hundreds of others already there; we were herded in and dismissed from our marching formation. To say that spirits were low at that point would again be an understatement and all sorts of possibilities were being suggested with pretty much everyone probably thinking that at worst this would be where we would meet our end mowed down, defenseless like so many rats in one big trap. That first night of captivity was bleak, we had no other option than to simply try and sleep where we had been dismissed from marching formation. Most were absolutely exhausted, finding sleep a temporary but welcome departure from the horrors of the past weeks and the stress of contemplating what horrors might be in store. I myself settled into an uneasy slumber, not what I would call proper sleep, waking several times to be brought suddenly back to reality and the harsh veracity of our miserable situation but never the less it was the first real sleep I'd experienced for weeks.

Very early next morning German trucks rolled into the field most loaded with roll upon roll of barbed wire with two loaded with large pots of soup. Negotiating with our officers working parties were formed to start the task of deploying the barbed wire all around the periphery of the field and orderly queues were also formed at the food trucks with each man being allowed a mess tin of watery vegetable soup and a ration of bread. Most muttered under their breath things like 'At least they're going to feed us before being shot' but some truths and news started filtering down from the officers who'd been interned in the field along with us regular soldiers. The general consensus was that we'd be used as a bargaining chip to help secure a surrender from Britain but not as big a bargaining chip as they'd hoped or planed for as we heard at that time of the thousands and thousands that had got away from Dunkirk, and the likelihood was that we'd be kept alive with POW labor camps our most probable fate.

It was blisteringly hot once the sun got up and again later in the morning trucks rolled up and the officers that had been interned with us in the field were segregated and taken away in the trucks under heavy German guard, this again set rumors abound as to our fate with everyone thinking well they'll just do whatever they like with us now, I imagine taking away our leadership was their goal in order to make us more easily subservient and less likely to rebel, after all we were still a large body of men and a serious threat if we could somehow be rearmed".

The Major butted into Syd's rendition commenting "Indeed Syd we missed a golden opportunity; how different things might have been had we had the option of dropping in airborne troops and weapons, such as we witnessed from the German attack at the Maginot Line. That was to become my mission or assignment you could say when I returned to Blighty as the speed, determination and ferocity of the airborne attack at the Maginot line was something that had certainly raised serious concerns with Churchill. Again, this is something I'll bring you up to speed on presently, but first go on with your rendition of events at St Valery, I can say for sure I can't imagine how demoralizing it must have been and I admire your strength of spirit and resolve to have coped with it so well. As I'm led to believe Syd, St Valery was the just the start, I'm keen to know of the march, 'The Hunger March' as I've heard it referred to and I need to be told of it so I feel I was actually there and experienced it myself".

The Hunger March.

Chapter 9.

"The Hunger March" exclaimed Syd "That is one way to describe it but I'd be more inclined to call it something much more contemptible or even appalling, but hunger was indeed one terrible aspect of it Ryton, hunger yes but more atrocious than that was the thirst, the burning torturous thirst." Syd speaking it still trying to maintain his newly acquired, officer power of command. Syd had to clear his throat before he could continue with his rendition, the mere thought of the march bringing back some truly horrendous dark memories.

Syd continued, "Two days Ryton they kept us in that field outside St Valery, constantly cramming in more and more to our, and as we learned later, other fields, as all the troops that had spilled out of the town onto the beaches and beyond were rounded up. Every addition to the field adding to our sense of hopelessness, although I have to say at that time spirits were still high despite our situation with the general feeling that yes we had been captured, yes we were in a dire situation but we felt we would show the Germans that we would not have our spirit and resolve broken. On the morning of the second day trucks arrived with food and once again orderly queues were formed to be rationed food in the form of watery soup that tasted as if it had been made with rotten potatoes and that was the last time we were fed by the Germans until we or at least those that survived the march got to our respective POW locations.

On the morning of the third day 'The March' began; Lorry loads of German foot soldiers and support vehicles arrived and we were brutally herded and formed into a three-file marching formation by 'German Infantrymen' commanding their instruction by jack boot, rifle butt, and bayonet point. We were commanded to start marching and the formed column started marching though the gated entrance to the field past an open backed German halftrack upon which a German Officer was stood next to a manned heavy caliber machine gun, addressing the moving column he was barking instructions through a megaphone as the column passed".

"The orders in very poor and heavily accented English being delivered over and over by the German Officer went something like this: - Keep moving and remain in file.

Anyone breaking formation will be classed as an attempted escapee and will be shot.
We will not leave anyone behind alive. if you can't keep up the pace you will be shot.
 You are marching to Germany and for you the war is over.
You will be put to work for the glory of the Reich, Hail Hitler.
These words repeated time and time again each time with seemingly more vigor as the column passed the gate. The barked directive had everyone worried, damned worried, everyone speculating whether this was indeed their true intention or whether we were just being duped and moved to a more convenient location for some other ghastlier processing or even execution.
The march itself was just day after day of seemingly unending torturing punishment, driven at a grueling pace again by jackboot and rifle butt, it seemed to most that we were not only being driven to physical breaking point but to psychological breaking point too. We were marched hard by day mostly taking back roads or at least off the main highways, we were driven hard without water or sustenance at all from the Germans and had it not been for the kindness of locals leaving

baskets of bread and buckets of water by the road side we would have all perished long before achieving our destination. Some guards were worse than others, some turned a blind eye to the food and water left by the road side but others would kick over the buckets of water depriving us marching prisoners of water on what were mostly blistering hot summer days.

By night we slept in open fields and suffered the cold and damp of the night, but we did at least in some cases manage to acquire some sustenance from vegetables and fruits being grown in the fields and managed to fill our flasks and canteens from muddied pools, streams, and ponds. Every morning following another uncomfortable night we were rallied at 05:00 and experienced the same brutal experience day after day after day. At night, some did take the opportunity to break free and flee the murder march, for true to their word many were executed at the side of the road for simply collapsing through exhaustion or for in the case of one of our band murdered, bayoneted to death for breaking rank to get bread from a farm girl at the side of the road in Belgium, that soldier being none other than Sergeant Blackshaw murdered for good intentions as all he'd wanted to do was to help his comrades".

Syd could feel himself welling up inside and struggling to contain his emotion at the thought of his murdered colleague and this must have been obvious to 'The Major' who butted in to relieve Syd from any embarrassing emotional displays.

"Sergeant Blackshaw? It strikes me this must have been one hell of a soldier Syd, please tell me more of this man, his background and career I feel I should know more of him as I imagine many will have known him and have had the greatest respect for him and remember Syd an officer hides his emotion this is something you must be aware of and always be in control of despite circumstances, remember Syd poise, dignity, and composure at all times, never forget it".

Syd was pleased at the interruption it did exactly what The Major had intended and gave Syd the chance to gather his composure.

Syd again started his rendition this time determined not to let emotion mar his performance specially in front of the man he was trying to imitate and who was to all intent and purpose, perhaps the calmest most confident and self-assured officer he had ever come across.

"Well Sergeant Blackshaw was indeed a respected soldier, born just before the turn of the century he was in his very early forties and had originated from the Newcastle area, he'd seen service in the trenches towards the end of the first world war and it was this experience that had gained him his rank in the Northumberland Fusiliers and the respect of those junior to him as well as our commanding officers in the territorial regiment to which we both belonged. Following the Great War, he'd settled in mid Northumberland finding work in the local mines, not the same one as me I might add although we were in the same Territorial battalion based in Alnwick Northumberland. The Sergeant or Jimmy to his friends was married and had three children, two sons and a daughter his wife being a school teacher. When we were first called up and sent for training and later when sent abroad and all the way through the Battle of France he'd been our mentor as well as our Sergeant, a true born leader and a soldier who commanded our respect and admiration, a man who just always seemed to know what to do. He wasn't a man of great physical stature being thin and wiry nevertheless he always seemed to have plenty of stamina. It was the surrender and the march that had been the start of his downfall. Unfortunately, he received, quite a knee injury from a purposely delivered rifle butt blow at St Valery most likely delivered because of his rank and again probably a demoralizing and weakening tactic applied by the Germans and it worked.

As the 'Murder March went on days after day in the heat of the mid-summer sun the men got progressively weaker each successive day. The start of the march was harsh, the pace was frantic, and our guards were brutal, we were driven hard, marching firstly through Formerie, then Forges-les Eaux, Doullens, and St Pol. On through France and into Belgium each day the men getting weaker and weaker, in strength, and more unclean and demoralized psychologically, yet outwardly everyone trying to project unbreakable spirit. Sergeant Blackshaw seemed to weaken quicker than the younger lads and compounded by his knee injury it became necessary to give him more and more assistance as the march went on with us closest comrades taking turns in pairs, helping him along, to the point where we had to practically carry him or at least bear most of his weight with his arms straddled over the shoulders of whoever was helping him. This must have played on his mind and I believe he must have realized that everyman needed all their own strength for themselves and he was becoming an ever-increasing burden to his comrades sapping the strength they'd need to survive. We'd seen already in the first week the fate of those that collapsed from exhaustion with a bayonet on the end of a German rifle being their exit ticket probably carried out as an exercise to save ammunition. On that particular day; the day of his execution it was particularly hot, in-fact blisteringly hot and just behind us in the column was one of the more obnoxious overzealous German guards who seemed to harbor a deep hatred of all things British. As we rounded a bend in the road we could see that there was a young girl at the side of the road holding a basket filled with bread crusts and apples, and she had arranged at the side of the road several buckets of water. News of our sad fate and plight must have been traveling in front of us on the local telegraph and we were starting to see this more and more often with baskets of fruit, bread, and water being left at the road side. As we got close to the girl Sergeant Blackshaw took it into his head to struggled free from his helpers and stumbled away free from the marching column. Taking the basket of apples and bread scraps from the girl he thanked her most kindly and probably using the last ounce of strength he had just before collapsing he thrust the basket skyward into the marching column where it was caught and the contents promptly distributed amongst the men who greedily gorged it down. A shout of angry disapproval in garbled German echoed out from the guard behind us and as the sergeant lay absolutely exhausted and motionless on the grassy roadside, the guard rushed up and with a lunging action stabbed him clean through the upper chest while uttering a stream of verbal German abuse. The blade must have penetrated through the sergeant's lung and his body retorted then he promptly spewed forth a torrent of blood from his mouth before his body relaxed back onto the grassy roadside; he gave out a gurgling noise, a probable indication that he was drowning on his own blood.

Many of us were so incensed, and instantly enraged at what we had just witnessed, almost instinctively we broke rank and lunged towards the German guard. He was quick to point his weapon towards our aggressive lunge and shout out HALT alerting other guards some with machine guns to run in our direction. Someone in the ranks shouted out 'As you were lads, as you were just keep marching, for hell sake don't waste his sacrifice, they'll mow us down like rats'. Reluctantly most realized that this shouted command, was at this time, and in this situation, the best course of action and some slower than others to readopt the march were beaten back to compliance by rifle butt and aggressively persuaded with kicks to readopt their formation and continue marching, this while the original guard kicked over the water buckets that the girl had had readied. The girl who'd been trying to help was instantly turned into a state of screaming hysteria, and turning around she was off in full flight, high tailing it back up the rough farm track where at the end of which she'd had the help arranged; the track probably back to her farm home. Although we had continued marching a little time after we heard a shot ring out and the general consensus was that one of the guards had taken a pot shot at the fleeing girl and I often wonder if those few crusts of bread and a few apples had cost her, her life as well as that of Sergeant Blackshaw, such a pretty young girl at that". With that Syd began to feel his voice starting to stammer a little and he paused again to regain his composure.

The Major interjected, "Syd that's one of the most heart rending stories I think I've ever heard, unbelievable that anyone could be so malicious, it's done nothing other than to strengthen my resolve to get back at this evil, evil, organization that could claim this sort of reprehensible act as glory for their despicable Reich and for their wretched Fuhrer. But my utmost respect and admiration must go to Sergeant Blackshaw for his final act of absolute selfless heroism, truly a great man. I hope one day we can get to honor his courage and ultimate sacrifice".

Syd by now the words from The Major regarding maintaining composure still fresh in his mind had gathered his emotions and was ready to go on with the briefing.

Syd cleared his throat and began, "Well Ryton the march went on but to say the loss of our Sergeant was demoralizing to our little band, would be an understatement, more a complete irony, perhaps even a travesty of what we believed to be the rules of war, it did however serve to strengthen our resolve and all talk after that was less of acceptance of our fate and more and more of how we could, hit back, escape, sabotage their war effort, I could say that the Sergeant's sacrifice to a great extent is why I'm here today and I know now why he did what he did, he must have known he was on his last legs and this was his last dying effort to cement our spirit and perhaps renew our resolve and by God it worked". (Author's Note. 'It did indeed cement Syd's resolve, that memory stayed with him to his dying day and to a great extent molded his character and made him the man he was for the rest of his life. The sense of fair play, honesty and integrity he instilled into his children was probably directly attributable to this and the other horrors of war he'd had to witness and for virtues he passed on I'll be eternally grateful.)

"It would be many, many, more days before we'd reach our final destination, the heat, the hunger, the burning thirst went on and on, each day seemingly worse and hotter than the one before then finally after marching some way through Holland we reached what would be our first transport. We were so weak by now that I can't even remember the name of the place we embarked the train, where we were crammed into box cars and locked in it was almost as horrendous as the march itself, but we were at least given some water, the Germans now probably realizing they had a usable asset in the form of forced labor which would be of great help in their war effort. I can't remember exactly how long we were in that transport, except to say it was the worst train journey of my life, and then ultimately we arrived at our destination near Bad-Sulzar in the middle of Germany and were then marched to our waiting camp Stalag IX C".

The Major had to sit back for a moment just to soak up the true gravity and magnitude of Syd's rendition. His thoughts were all over the place, he thought a little of home, of his own course through the war, of all the close escapes he'd had, of the plight, the suffering, and the sacrifice that thousands upon thousands of men and women just such as Syd and he and Sergeant Blackshaw and of the farm girl from Syd's story. He dwelled a little as he thought of the collective selfless sacrifice that so many must have made, and it humbled him, it truly humbled him almost to the point where he found himself close to tears and thinking of the advice he'd only just given to Syd he quickly forced a regaining of composure by voicing the statement. "Syd, I am truly humbled and in awe of the sacrifice and contribution you and your comrades have made and I do mean that most sincerely, truly humbled indeed, your most recent account has made me more committed than ever to get back at the enemy and thwart their despicable plan we must strive to make a success of this operation and nip their plan in the bud, let's press on. I imagine all you need to go over now is your transit through the POW system and Syd I'm most intrigued, just how you managed to attain a position in the Oflags, with you having been a miner I would have thought you'd have ended up in a working camp somewhere employed in some sort of mining operation. Let's start with your arrival at Stalag IXC and take it from there. I'll need to know precise dates and such like just in case I happen to bump into a former internee of a previous camp of yours and he recognizes you or us you could say, but more so in case I'm questioned on it". As you can imagine I must remain completely in disguise, at all times even to officers and men that I meet following the swap this morning and of course it must be the same for you if any enlisted men here question you, or are in the least bit suspicious you must remain in character and never let your true identity slip to anyone and I repeat anyone"!

P.O.W.

Chapter 10.

Syd readied himself to continue with his rendition, he had all his dates and locations committed to memory and hoped he didn't get any wrong. The Major was going to have to commit them to his memory in a very short space of time and get them right if he was ever questioned on them.

The Major ever more astonished at Syd's rendition commented "Right now Syd I wish we'd spent a lot more time getting to know each other before the swap I realize now that I was a bit presumptuous to assume your life and military history would be easy to emulate".

Syd had regained his composure now, he took a deep breath and began. "Well Ryton I think it best to answer your question first, the one regarding me being here in the Oflags.

Syd began; "Upon arrival at the Bad Sulza on July 12th we were herded off the box car transport, everyone absolutely exhausted and close to starvation, we were marched to Stalag IX-C on the hottest of summer mornings. Everyone was anxious to find out what our new accommodations were going to be like and somewhat relieved to find out it was at least a solidly built brick and concrete building and it was easy to see it had been hurriedly prepared to accommodate prisoners. The windows had all been barred with very thick wire mesh, the type used to keep animals in, and there were rudimentary barbed wire fences arranged around the perimeter of the building which were later made much more substantial. There were already hundreds upon hundreds of Polish POW's there captured from Germany's conquest of Poland together with one or two other nationalities. There were also some British, French and Belgians, already there captured from the Battle of France and from the retreat to Dunkirk. We were crammed into filthy rooms around 150 in each room measuring 120 feet by 60 feet but at last mercifully, and I mean mercifully 'some of the men on their last legs' we were fed, bread crusts and cabbage soup and we were allowed as much water as we needed. That meal tasted like a banquet, a banquet fit for a king, or so it felt and as it turned out that or potato soup along with a bread ration was pretty much going to be our staple diet for the duration of our stay.

The first two days we went through an organizing process or you could say a registration process with the Germans wanting to catalog and list prisoners into their differing categories of usability. As part of this process each of us were given a form to fill in and these were to give the Germans some idea of our previous skills and where these skills could be best, put to work, for the greater good of The Reich and for the Fatherland. The form consisted of questions pertaining to name, rank, regiment, marital status, previous civilian occupation, even interests and special skills. We were told anyone refusing to fill in the form would be sent directly to the nearby salt or potassium mining operation and it was in our best interests to fill out the form. We all or at least our little group who were mostly Northumbrian coal miners got together and discussed what we were going to put on the form and after some hours of debate concluded that putting any mention of coal mining on the forms would see us sent straight to some Nazi mining operation and we also concluded that considering our treatment on the march then our life expectancy would be short and the chances of escape minimal. A long discussion brought our little group to the conclusion that if we were to put down that we were coal trimmers and by that, I mean people employed to shovel coal around in ship's holds to get the trim and load of the vessel correct before sailing then we'd be sent to a port somewhere from which the chances of escape would be much greater. I wholeheartedly disagreed with this thinking to myself that if the Germans thought our only skill was shoveling coal then that would be our assurance of being directly assigned to the mines. There was a little disagreement but everyone agreed they must make the decision themselves and fill out the form whichever way they saw fit.

So, after some thought, I indicated on the form that my previous employment had been as a counter assistant in the local cooperative society menswear department, you know fitting male clients for suits of clothes, taking inside leg measurement, advising on dress etiquette, all that sort of thing. The sad truth is though that I don't and have never even owned a suit of my own never mind advise or measure up anyone for one, as I always preferred to spend the little spare cash I was allowed to keep on my hobby, that being cycling, and it is bicycling that allowed me to join and be part of the Territorial Regiment in Alnwick which was a 20-mile round trip, on my trusty BSA bicycle, two times a week. So, again after some thought I also indicated on the form that my hobby was cycling, bicycle repair, and maintenance. My thoughts ran along the lines that the Germans would think me, being a clothing assistant, with no manual work experience, far too soft to be of any use in the mines but thinking, I had some mechanical aptitude, might think me better placed in manufacture, or perhaps in a mechanical warehouse or maybe even something clerical or office based, maybe even something in their military uniform departments".

"Cunning indeed Syd, cunning indeed", interjected The Major.

"Thank you, Ryton, and yes I thought it would be far better to end up in some sort of semi-skilled employment where my contribution might be valued and from where my chance of escape would be far greater. Unfortunately, after six weeks in Stalag IX-C we were all assigned to a working camp in Eisenach so we all, concluded, that the time and effort taken and detail we'd entered into our POW registration had been a wasted effort and the Germans were just going to use us for what even purpose they wanted and had no real interest in our previous employment or at least not in what we thought must have been, fairly commonplace skills to them.

We were marched on the 31st of August and interned in the working camp at Eisenach and found we'd been assigned to construction work on the Reich's new road building program which were made known to us as autobahns. The work consisted of leveling and preparing ground, and laying concrete foundations for the new roads. As it turned out it was a little better than we had at first expected and consisted of 10 hours work per day with half an hour break mid-morning and the same at mid-day. Accommodations were very similar to Stalag IX-C that being very, very, rudimentary with flea infested straw mattresses installed into three tier bunks so in effect we were crammed into rooms like sardines. Reveille was four thirty and roll-call at six o-clock. We had a one-hour march in our respective working parties which got us to our destination right on time for starting time of seven o-clock. We were issued with our food ration once per day in the evening consisting of German soup and bread and my usual habit was to eat everything on issue and then wait 24 hours for the next. The only time I differed from this was on my 21st birthday when I kept my soup from the previous evening ration and ate the soup at lunch time and had the bread ration at two o-clock. I remember thinking 'what a way to spend a 21st birthday' and wondered what I might have been doing had it not been for the war and my predicament and I concluded that I've most probably would have spent it doing a shift down the pit but I might of at least had some sort of birthday celebration with my mother and girlfriend. I did feel sad and bitter for a while but soon snapped out of thinking that at least I was still alive and probably a lot better off that some who'd been captured.

It came as a great surprise to me when I was informed on the 27th July 1941 that I was to be recalled back to Stalag IX-C and I was even more surprised when I was informed that I was to be sent to Oflag X-C near to the city of Lubeck in the north and I arrived there on the 4th September 1941. As I mentioned a complete surprise and seemingly as a direct result of the information that I'd entered into the POW registration form. The work was in stark contrast to that which I become used to at the Stalag, and consisted of looking after the British Officers, sweeping their room floors, washing tables, drawing For whatever reason we British POW's, officers and enlisted men, together with those from two other camps were moved and amalgamated into a single camp at Warburg right in the middle of Germany. We left Oflag X-C on the 8th October 1941 and arrived at Oflag VI-B on the 10th October 1941.

My duties remained the same but as a result of my previous experience in supporting break out attempts my time in this camp became very interesting. We and by that, I mean the Officers mounted a mass break out attempt code naming it Operation Olympia also known as the Warburg Wire Job and saw me, being ideally situated as outside working party, helping in constructing and concealing 2 each 12 foot ladders and 2 each scaling duckboard bridges made to bridge the double fences and made mostly from wooden bed slats. It was on the 30 August 1942 that the escape attempt was made and started with a Major Gunn fusing the perimeter flood lights, then 41 prisoners including myself, carrying the ladders, charged the fences and under constant machine gun fire from enraged guards in the tower, were able to scale the barbed wire fence and climb over the duckboard bridges to the other side. Unfortunately, it being officers first as I waited my turn to scale the ladder and probably as a result of over zealousness, the ladder I was to climb collapsed due to too many and too much weight on it at one time. It was unfortunate indeed and as a result of the 41 officers and men only 28 escaped the camp. The ones left inside the camp including me were able to scuttle back to our huts and evaded detection by the Germans.

To say the Germans were incensed would again be one of my understatements, and throwing their whole system of security into disarray with the panic to recapture the escaped prisoners, this again prompted another move for the British Officers and me. We never heard how many or even if any made it back to Blighty but not all 28 returned to captivity and that was a huge boost to morale.

The 10th September 1942 saw the entire British contingent moved again, this time here to Oflag VII-B and we arrived here at our new camp on 12th September 1942 with the sternest of warnings from 'The Bosch' that any further mass breakout attempts would be met with the sternest of consequences. This I might add was like waving a red flag at a bull and served only to reinforce the resolve and determination to mount future attempts".

"So then Syd seems like you've led one hell of a checkered career, if you could call it that, throughout your captivity as a POW, and I suppose then the stories of you being involved in the mass breakout from here last year must be true then"? interrupted the Major keen to get an account straight from the horse's mouth of the mass breakout he'd heard so much about since he'd got to the Oflag.

The Tunnel.

Chapter 11.

"Yes indeed Ryton," went on Syd, "As I mention arriving at this camp and with the sternest of warnings issued from the Germans not to attempt any more mass escapes it was practically like being issued with a challenge and a challenge to which we rose almost immediately. A tunnel was proposed to be excavated from next door, block II and was to run from the block's latrines northward almost 100 feet to a chicken coop on the other side of the perimeter. It was known before the start that it would be a difficult mining project with the ground running uphill and the nature of the ground being rocky with soft earth in-between, so this is where I came in with my previous mining experience. Not being one of the officers I was over the moon to be selected as the ideal choice to spearhead driving the tunnel and became what you could call a mining mentor not only digging myself but passing on my knowledge of mining to the digging teams. As mentioned the digging was far tougher than we'd ever thought it would be, with the ground being very rocky, and everything in the way of digging implements having to be either fashioned from something else, acquired from bribed locals working in the camp, or simply done by hand. Because of the nature of the ground the whole length of the tunnel had to be propped, planked, and shored, and for this we utilized anything we could get our hands on with the wooden bunks again sacrificing a lot of their slats, and thicker timbers coming from roof spaces underfloor spaces or anywhere we could get away with taking it without it being obvious, even wood meant for our wood stoves was used as props. The Germans at one point did find spoil at the south side of the camp where we'd disposed of it underneath some huts so knowing there must be tunneling going on somewhere they searched and searched for the tunnel but never suspected because of the nature of the ground that it would be at the north end of the camp and concentrated their searches at the south side finding nothing. We started preparations for the tunnel December 1942, firstly cutting a trapdoor next to a toilet so the entrance could be concealed then beneath the trapdoor we excavated vertically down and dug out a sizable chamber from which all tunneling could be managed, a little bit like a regular mine really. We utilized sections of stove chimney pipe joined together to form a ventilation system and used the same system as in coal mines to pull air through the entire mine rather than to try to push it in. The stove pipes were arranged all the way to the face and a manually operated bellows type pump was operated from the chamber under the trapdoor and this pulling or exhausting air right from the face, served to pull air all the way through the tunnel and stop the air becoming foul.

Tunneling from the chamber began in earnest at the end of January 1943 and almost straight away difficulties were encountered with large boulders obstructing the tunnels progress. The first a large boulder protruding down from the roof and this we nicknamed 'The Coffin', the second around 50 feet in we called 'The Belly Crawl', this was where two large rocks in the ceiling and one in the floor created a space of around only 14 inches through which we had to crawl. The third was a huge boulder right in the tunnel path and with no other option we had to tunnel around it in both directions and join up on the other side, this we named 'Piccadilly Circus'. Digging was frantic with the digging teams of four, five or even six men working a shift pattern to keep things rolling. One man at the face a second behind loading spoil into a box on a wheeled cart, two men pulling the spoil all the way back to the chamber, then loading it into bags to be disposed of above ground, and another operating the ventilation. There were a few hiccups as the tunnel approached its end, digging into a huge boulder and only being a few feet short of the objective it was decided to stop there and dig upwards, but pretty much by the end of May we were ready to go".

"That's very impressive Syd", interrupted the Major, "So the Germans never really got wind that anything was going on then? Brilliant that you were able to put your mining experience to such good use Syd and I'm so pleased you've now brought me up to speed on it, I don't suppose I'll bump into any officers that were involved in the escape as the German recruitment campaign is aimed almost completely at the enlisted men, regular fighting soldiers is what they are aiming for but it's still good to have all this knowledge, just in case I need it, please Syd carry on". Syd pleased that his efforts were being recognized continued with a bit of a smile on his face, "There was some conspiracy in the camp from either a guard or perhaps even a prisoner colluding with the Germans as notes were found around the camp highlighting the fact that escaping prisoners in civilian clothes could be legally shot as spies. The notes had been signed as 'A German friendly to the British', but despite these and a tip off to the Germans that a tunnel was being dug from the staircase below block II, the Germans searched but never found anything and concluded that the tip off had been a hoax. Great efforts were made to try and discover the identity of the note writer and the informant but despite repeated efforts including hand writing comparisons no one was ever identified and so after one or two postponed dates because of weather, namely wind needed to cover the sound of escape not happening, on the evening of the 3rd of June, 65 officers had been selected to escape and readied to go. So, you could say myself and a naval pretty officer who'd helped with the dig were numbers 66 and 67 although we were never allocated a number as we were a pivotal part of the escape plan.

Great preparations had been made, we were all wearing civilian clothing, or uniforms altered to look like civilian clothes, everyone had maps that had been produced in the camp, some had bags and cases and such like to make us look more like authentic travelers. Some had compasses, forged documents, and some even speaking very convincing German, everyone felt sure that at least some would make it back to Blighty or if not cause one hell of a stir in the effort to do so.

Harry the naval petty officer you could say was the first and the last man scheduled to escape as he was to break through at the exit and then stay there to help the officers out of the tunnel. I was unfortunately the last man scheduled to escape, although not on the list as I mentioned, it had been our job Harry's and mine right at the start of the evening to de-rig the ventilation pipework and stack it back in the chamber, to create a larger crawl space for the officers to get through while wearing coats and pushing cases and such before them.

As I mentioned Harry and I also had the additional responsibility of being first and last through the tunnel and once I was out we were to use pre prepared timbers and planks to conceal and cover the discharge end of the tunnel so it might be possible to use it a second time as the same was to be done by others at the latrine end to keep the entire tunnel hidden It took around 20 minutes or so for each man to crawl through the tunnel and the escape went on right through the night and into the early hours of the next morning. By the time it was my turn, the last man to go through the tunnel the air was beginning to get, foul, pretty foul indeed and I was so relieved to get out at the other end, and breath the clean fresh air on a warm but windy summer morning. I exited the tunnel to find that although a few feet short we were still on the right side of the chicken coop fence where we needed to be and my escape partner Harry the naval petty officer was beckoning me to join him secluded in a hedge on the other side of the coop. He'd been busy and had all the bits and pieces we needed, set out at the entrance, these had been handed out to him by successive escaping officers. Checking that we were OK to start and still hadn't been detected, and with no sirens having gone off we went back to the tunnel exit to where the pre-preparade timbers, and homemade shovel were arranged and we feverishly set about putting the planks and props in place and covered over the exit with dirt that had been pushed out when forming the exit. I was pleased that all the chickens were at roost for the evening and still in the roost that time in the morning, although from time to time they did make some noise but on the whole, they remained calm, it did go through my mind a few times being familiar with chicken coops back home that once startled a bunch of alarmed chickens could make one hell of a noise and I did question the logic of planning the exit in amongst the chickens. Although not on the officers list, as I've mentioned me being number 67 to exit the tunnel, that was how many escaped that day, sixty-five officers and two enlisted men. Most all who'd exited the tunnel and made their escape before us were already dispersed and long gone, the plan being for escapees to travel in groups of two or three and most would have probably headed south with the intention of making the Swiss border. We also knew that being the last to make our escape and having to take the time to conceal the exit to the tunnel as best we could we'd have far less opportunity to put some distance between the camp and ourselves once the escape was discovered so we decided that we'd head north then east and then try and hide in the woods until the heat died down. We hoped that after a few days we'd then be able to head south and our objective was Switzerland".

"Sounds like it was a great plan Syd, but what went wrong, obviously you're still here"? mused The Major.

"Well we had the disadvantage as I said of being first but more significantly of being last out the tunnel and we thought that German efforts to search for prisoners would be focused to the south, but the one thing we didn't count on was dogs being used to track us down, dogs having been trained specifically for the purpose. We probably had several hours start before the alarms sounded and the Germans were alerted to the escape but they must have gotten the dogs into the camp to get the scent or possibly they found our exit or may-be they were even tipped off by the collaborator as to the tunnels location, the same collaborator who'd posted the warning notes perhaps. Essentially, we were literally hunted and tracked down like animals and I imagine we having just dug fresh earth mixed with a good percentage of chicken shyte in the chicken coop this must have given the dogs a pretty good and strong scent to follow."

"Careful" interrupted The Major, "You slipped back into a colloquialism there not the sort of word an officer would use".

Syd embarrassed a little continued. "We'd gone into some thick woods probably around 6 or so miles to the north and planned to hide there until the following evening so we could use the cover of darkness to then move to the east but as I mentioned we knew the game was up as soon as we heard the approaching dogs, they were excited and barking like mad and obviously hot on our trail. We quickly planned to try and find some water, a stream perhaps to cover our trail and aid our escape but to no avail. The dogs sniffed us out with relative ease and despite we trying to make a run for it, off the leash the pack of German Shepherd dogs soon caught, attacked and pinned us down until the armed guards caught up and we were brutally and I mean brutally taken back into captivity. That was the worst feeling in the world having been free for just a few short hours but we hoped and better hoped that we might have drawn some of the heat and given others a better chance to get away.

At first, we thought we'd be simply returned to the camp but that wasn't to be and we were literally frog marched out of the woods thrown into the back of, and taken by truck to the nearby Willibaldsburg Castle and locked up in its dungeon like basement rooms, the very first of the escapees to have been caught".

(Author's Note....... Although Syd did not dislike dogs following this experience he could never warm to them and never owned or allowed his family to own one even in his later years when it was suggested he might get one as a companion)

"That's one hell of a story Syd and must have been so disappointing, I've heard all the officers ended up at 'Colditz Oflag IV-C', tell me a little about that?" suggested The Major.

Syd was begging to get the feeling that The Major was asking the road he already, pretty much knew but recalled that The Major had mentioned he'd wanted to hear it from the 'Horse's Mouth' so again he set himself away with ever growing verbal confidence.

"Well our first experience of what felt like the castle dungeon was perhaps one reminiscent of its historical past that being one of interrogation and perhaps not torture but something very close to it, you could call it extremely rough handling. This went on for some time and the longer it went on the more we hoped that it must mean others had gotten away. They wanted to know names, escape routes, descriptions, who'd done the planning all that sort of stuff, but despite the treatment we remained silent even though our treatment became harsher as time went on we were determined to give the others the best possible chance and knew we must remain silent, come what may. Then to our utter dismay, the next pair of captured prisoners joined us in the dungeons and then slowly more and more, as group after group were recaptured and the rough treatment and interrogation turned to them. We were fed as the days went on but only just enough to keep us alive, just stale bread and water and not much of it.

We spent a total of fourteen days in the castle dungeon and eventually all 65 of the officers were captured and although initially we felt as if we'd failed ultimately it was heralded as a success, being as we'd tied up vital German resources and time with the search to recapture us. The SS, regular German army units, the Hitler Youth, the police, armed civilian volunteers, the prison guards, literally hundreds and hundreds if not thousands of personnel and valuable resources. Some were captured as they travelled through villages, some at railway stations, some on the open road and even as we some tracked and hunted down using dogs.

When all 67 of us were in custardy the decision was taken for everyone to be sent to Oflag IV-C the infamous Colditz Castle which we knew to be for persistent escapees, quite literally it was the 'Bad Boys Oflag' from which it was thought escape to be almost impossible. The Castle was certainly an impressive formidable building you could even say an impregnable medieval fortress, not ideal as a POW facility, although well-guarded, but mostly by men either too old or too young for the front. Multiple roll calls throughout the day meant prisoners had little time to plot escapes and life there I would imagine would have been a lot tougher than that here in Eichstatt. There is not really that much further to tell of Colditz as once there, we were further processed and for both Harry and me our stay was very short. It had been decreed by the Wermacht that because of the nature, and supposedly penal status or classification of Colditz the officers interned there-in would not have the privilege of subordinates or lower ranks interned with them to improve their lot, and make their life easier, or at least that is what were told and consequently after only a few days both Harry and I were returned here to VII-B, and that Ryton brings us just about up to date. We did however find out while at Colditz seemingly from radios they had smuggled and hidden there and from received BBC broadcasts that the allies had landed in France on 6th June so we returned here to Eichstatt happy in the knowledge that perhaps the tides of war were turning and there existed the distinct possibility of a not too far in the future, end to the war". Once we returned here to find that news had already circulated around the POW population there did seem to be a bit of a change of heart in some. Many thought they'd done their bit and now the best plan was to sit things out, keep their heads down and just wait for the allies to liberate the camps. Others went the opposite way thinking the more they could disrupt things behind the lines the sooner the war would end and news of the allied invasion of France only served to increase their determination to escape. For me as I've said Ryton that is why I'm sitting here now, the thought of lads switching sides now after the atrocities I've witnessed and actually helping the German war effort goes completely against the grain, even if they are to some extent being duped by lies, proper-gander and bribery."

"Commendable, Syd highly commendable", conjectured the Major "That's one hell of a story and a lot would say you've done your bit, done your bit and a whole lot more, and for me Syd my thoughts are the same, I think we should not only infiltrate this disgrace but do everything we can to disrupt, or even sabotage their initiative, I can imagine no greater travesty than allied soldiers coming up against and having to combat British and Allied soldiers wearing Nazi uniforms, the thought of that literally makes my piss boil! And when I say boil I mean BOIL! But time is getting on here Syd, it's my turn now to bring you up to speed with my experiences and fate after I returned to good old Blighty, from then and right up to now, so pin your ears back Syd and listen intently as we'll pretty much only have enough time to go over this once, before I must take your place and skedaddle off to Stalag VII-A. Oh and congratulations Syd that's one hell of an impersonation of me and my officer attributes, now let's get on".

The Call to Jump.

Chapter 12.

"Well Syd I'll start right from my return to Blighty, following my lucky escape from Saint Nazaire, I'll try to be brief but include all the key events. So, starting from, disembarking the Naval Destroyer in Falmouth on the morning of the 19th June 1940 all officers that had made it back to Britain were quickly separated from the men and spirited away for a debrief of exactly what had gone on. This was the intelligence services trying to glean every and any bit of information they could, to build up a bigger picture of exactly what had gone wrong and indeed if anything had gone right. I was interviewed by some very, very, high ranking officers, and I mean very high ranking and, in particular they were very interested in the events right at the start of the German offensive, and perhaps more so they were interested in the events that had led up to it. The events to which Syd I believe we were both privy and that being the disastrous phoney war and our failed opportunity to smash the German defenses when they were at their weakest. I was still incensed by the events I'd just experienced at Saint Nazaire and the loss of the lancastria and I believe I was more than ready to give vent and point blame, at someone or indeed anyone but realized that out of all this chaos they were simply trying to make sense of, and learn from our mistakes. So, taking measure of my experiences and trying to convey some sort of wisdom gleaned from them, I stressed to the interviewing officers that in my opinion our biggest blunder, and I still believe it to this day, had been not attacking the Siegfried line when German defenses had been at their weakest, as they would have been thinly stretched with most of their divisions committed to the invasion of Poland. Incredibly that was something like an eight-month period following the invasion of Poland on September 1st, 1939 when British and French troops on the Maginot Line probably could have turned the tides of the war around and ended it before it had ever really began. I was probably being over critical, perhaps even super critical of decisions taken by the war office at levels way above my head and standing, and to be honest probably sticking my neck out way too far, but that's me Syd, brutal, critical, honesty is one of my traits so good or bad Syd, I hope you can carry off mimicking it, as essentially, I refuse to suffer fools and don't mind telling them so.

I went on to discuss the German use of airborne troops and how successful I'd been led to believe they'd been when the Germans had invaded the Netherlands and also went on to suggest that we were way behind German innovation and some of their new tactics of war, blitzkrieg, air support, dive bombers spearheading their offensive, vastly superior tanks and infantry following close behind, airborne troops, parachute and glider borne and more than anything the new mindset of the German assault trooper more so of the parachute troops, and their dogged determination to succeed and then better succeed at whatever cost, and I even suggested we should at the soonest opportunity create our own airborne divisions and we should do it with the utmost urgency. This Syd is where you could say my bluff was called.

Seemingly I was not alone in my recognition of just how useful and versatile airborne troops could be and in imagining the host of operations where they could be used and prove devastating on chosen targets and operations way behind enemy lines, Winston Churchill had recognized this too. He'd recognized and been impressed by the German use of paratroopers in operations in Norway that had experienced varying degrees of success, and Netherlands where they'd been dropped in front of advancing armored divisions to secure bridge heads in the German Blitzkrieg. He's also been most impressed with the German use of glider borne troops when they'd been used to neutralize, the thought to be impregnable Belgian fortress at Eben-Emael on 10th May 1940 by a comparatively small force of just 85 soldiers. This allowed the German forces to enter Belgium unhindered by fire from the fort and press on almost unopposed through Belgium.

Prompted by my interest and me preaching the potential of airborne troops, the panel of high ranking officers interviewing me asked if I'd be interested in volunteering to join a newly forming regiment, and a parachute battalion being trained for a top-secret mission under a directive from Winston Churchill himself. Syd, I could hardly refuse, in fact I was delighted at the prospect, and within 24 hours I'd been rushed through the reception, and repatriation process, kitted out with new uniform and so forth and I was on a train and on my way to London for an interview, I could hardly believe my luck although I must admit I'd thought a little bit of leave might not have gone a miss. Hardly an interview but more an organizational assembly, a setup of hierarchy, a pep-talk from Winston Churchill himself, and ultimately the formation of a regiment is what took place, that being the formation on the 22nd of June 1940 of a proposed corps of 5000 parachute troops who'd be trained for special airborne operations with an emphasis on behind enemy lines and covert operations. Without delay I was sent to Ringway Airport near Manchester and my objective was to assist in setting up and to implement the facilities, training, and command structure we'd need to train specialist parachute soldiers and within less than a month the first volunteers for special air service had started to arrive for training".

Suddenly a huge penny dropped in Syd's subconscious at the mention of Winston Churchill and he felt himself rambling a little and blurting out, "That's one hell of a remit to try and imitate Ryton especially bearing in mind you've met Churchill himself, I'm a little concerned that someone in the know will find it easy to trip me up on key points", suggested Syd, showing more than a little outward concern as the gravity and complexity of what he was about to take on hit home pretty damned hard and he started displaying obvious signs of panic and self-doubt. He realized that not knowing a dot about specialized airborne operations he'd be exposed in an instant by someone who did, not only that the high-powered people the Major had rubbed shoulders with that was another concern and the mention of Winston Churchill had him in a positive tail spin. "That's where we've been a little bit cunning and I'd hoped we wouldn't need to go down this road but here is an option that I think will soften the load a little for you Syd" replied the Major quickly recognizing that Syd was having doubts regarding his ability to carry out the plan. "We've or more precisely the few in the camp that know of this plan have been making it known around the camp not only to the other Officers but to the Germans as well that poor Major Willis has started to go a little doolally, you know, combat stress, shell shock, prisoner futility syndrome, call it what you will, and that's why I'm being rather vague and not going into great detail. Syd; I know it takes a very clever man to imitate the fool but I believe it will be for the greater good if questioned on a key point that you go off into some sort of self-imposed distant ramble giving garbled mention to a few key points than it would be for you to memorize a thousand and one key facts and be in danger of execution for knowing them and even worse of giving them up under torture if you were ever found out, and don't forget it works both ways Syd , I'm off imitating you and probably know less of a mineworkers lot than does the Lord Mayor of London. Besides that, Syd we too have been putting out a few rumors regarding yourself or indeed now myself to the Germans and it is these rumors regarding your increasing anti-officer attitude and anti-British ideology together with our request to have you transferred and replaced that has prompted the Germans to send you or I suppose more to the point me to Stalag VII-A where we know recruiting for the Free-Corps is taking place. So, come what may Syd exchange or not we are both going to have to deal with the consequences of what we've started here and we must see it through". The little jolt from the Major was just what Syd had needed, he was back on track and as the Major went on, Syd's mind went into overdrive regarding how he was going to carry off impersonating someone just starting to descend into the pits of mental instability. Not something he hadn't seen at least a hundred times already and indeed had to deal with on a day to day basis but at least this being an option made him feel better.

The Major's face started to get a little sterner and he started to lecture again, "Right Syd now comes the nitty gritty and when I say that take it by no means lightly, the information I'm about to divulge to you is dangerous, damned dangerous, if the Germans were to find out; basically about my past and operations I've been involved in then it would almost certainly mean torture and indeed execution, and I believe you've experienced some German rough handling already so, better start getting good at acting the fool or at least someone a little mentally unstable and from this moment on you are Major Gordon Willis in every way shape and form and never and I repeat never admit you're not, to anyone and I mean anyone, even those you think might be in the know. Remember Hitler's directive Syd, immediate execution for any special forces found operating behind the line and again what I'm about to tell you will help you realize the reason behind that stern and deplorable directive".

Biting and Beyond.

Chapter 13.

"Well firstly Syd, let's start with the idea behind the formation of the parachute regiments and as I've already mentioned was the result of a directive right from Winston Churchill himself. Winston had been so impressed with airborne assaults carried out by the Germans that he was quick to recognize we were lagging way behind in this theater of war and he also knew just how valuable elite specialized troops could be in special missions, surprise attacks, essentially anything that could be done swiftly and with deadly force behind enemy lines, before the enemy had a chance to prepare or even possibly react. He knew too that the Germans had years of experience with their parachute forces having been in existence for six years or so and also, they having had the benefit of training by the Russian Military and their paratroop forces.

My mission initially was to help take the new volunteers to the parachute regiments and get them trained and up to speed and form them into an elite fighting force. Syd, we started with so very little, no procedures, no experience to draw from, out dated and unsuitable aircraft (Whitney Mark III bombers) from which to train, not even any new equipment having to make do with old parachutes, but what we did have was dedication, and a gravel in the gut desire to succeed and strike at the enemy any way we could.

After several months of training, developing new equipment, procedures and tactics we had amassed a few hundred soldiers all with the necessary skills and the 11th Special Air Service Battalion, was formed.

It was February the following year that would see the battalion's first action code named Operation Biting, and to be honest Syd was carried out with most of the men taking part having the least training and the least experience. It was however after the event heralded as an overwhelming success and put the parachute regiment and special forces right bang center on the map.

I think at this point I should tell you a little of our first objective and of the urgency as to why we had to do it. Firstly, Syd I know you'll probably have never heard of radar, and to be honest I'm not a technical boffin either, but radar is a means of transmitting radio waves into the air and bouncing them off aircraft. This equipment can then pick up and see these reflections and from this information can determine where and even how many aircraft there are in the air at any given time or at least that's what they tell me. Like a lot of things 'The Germans' were thought to be way ahead of us Brits in the development of this technology and intelligence from reconnaissance aircraft had identified several sites where installations had been built and it was these that was thought to be the reason why we were suffering increasing losses on bombing missions with the enemy using this technology; as it had the capability to provide the exact whereabouts to guide fighter aircraft directly to our planes and of course resulting in them being shot down".

Syd was gob smacked he hadn't realized anything like this existed but was pleased he was at least being informed of it and of the Major's part in helping to neutralize it.

"Syd, we simply had to do something about it" continued the Major; "weeks of planning went into the mission. As I mentioned I'll not go into great detail, and to be honest the true nature of the raid is something we are still trying to keep a lid on, but I'll outline the general plan as there is the possibility you'll bump into someone from the raid as several guys didn't make it back to Blighty and there's a good chance, they were taken prisoner of war and I'd hate yours or more so our cover to be blown inadvertently by one of our own men recognizing us and you not being in the know. If it does happen then just remind who so ever it may be of our code, and leave it at that with perhaps a small tell-tale remark that will leave them in no doubt as to who you or we are and as to what that remark will be Syd you'll have to play that one by ear but at least you'll be able to draw from what I'm going to tell you now.

To continue Syd, the radar installation we were to attack was at Bruneval in northern France on the channel coast just a short way inland from the cliffs and the beach. The external equipment was situated near to a small villa and housed inside the villa was the power and control components and it was these that had priority. We attacked it on the night of 27th February 1942 after some anxious waiting and several weather-related delays. The mission was kept so secret the men didn't even know the target location right up to the last minute and all our plans had been devised from scale models and some very clever photographic techniques and training had revolved around simulations out in the field.

The assignment was to look like a sabotage mission but, in reality, it was to steal unique components from the equipment and get them back home so the boffins could work out exactly how they worked and devise ways to block its use and to aid us in this task we took along an expert in radar, whom I might say was ill prepared and far from readied for the mission. The site was to be left wrecked so all evidence of parts theft would be covered up in the devastation that ensued.

The system was a two component installation with a mattress mast type arrangement and the other a large dish like apparatus and this dish thing together with its operating equipment was our main objective.

We had trained with the navy and had practiced our evacuation many time and landing craft were to be used to get us off the beach and back to gun boats. The mission went ahead with three sections one to attack the villa where the main radar components would be, one to destroy and take parts from the outside radar assemblies and my section which was to secure the beach and take out a machine gun nest which would block the route back to the beach for the evacuating men. When we jumped into the theater my section unfortunately ended up short numbered as half the section ended up being dropped a mile or two off target, but unaware of their plight my men and I set about securing the beach as we had been ordered, fortunately the rest of the section had quickly grouped, got their bearings and had high tailed it to our objective which then turned out to be a two pronged attack which worked out very well and just in time, following a frenzied fire fight, the machine gun was taken out, and the beach was secured ready for the other sections who'd successfully completed their mission. They evacuated with a prisoner, and key components from the radar installation, some of them very heavy and taking considerable effort to haul along on trolleys, and all this under very heavy fire from the Germans who were now in hot pursuit having deployed from a barracks nearby. I might add the other objective to destroy the site and make it look like an act of sabotage had been carried out. When we had all regrouped on the beach it was found we couldn't contact the navy as they'd had to withdraw further out to sea to keep out of the way of a German patrol boat and we were forced to use flares, in an attempt, to alert them to our situation. Luckily the navy were on the ball and seeing the flare realized what was going on and our evacuation craft were dispatched. Under heavy fire and I mean heavy fire six landing craft returning Bren gun fire to the cliff tops as they came in made it to the beach to a barrage of welcoming comments from us. Commandos had been placed onboard and it was these chaps that were returning fire to the Germans, and had to a great extent kept them pinned down and behind cover allowing us a disorganized but successful withdrawal from the beach. All six craft had made it to the beach in a very confused fashion and all six eventually evacuated the beach with all mission objectives having been achieved. You could say our objective was achieved, and achieved with devastating results, it gave the enemy a good hard kick in the pants and made them realize they couldn't sit cozy on the other side of the channel. Although we were never told exactly what we had achieved the mission was heralded as a huge success and I would imagine it was this first raid and other successive raids that infuriated, and prompted Hitler to issue his decree that any special forces soldiers captured behind enemy lines on covert missions were to be given no quarter, no prisoner of war status and were to be immediately executed as spies. So, Syd this is what I mentioned earlier and how important it is to remain in absolute character, never give up you true identity to anyone, and although I've given over no names you should at least have enough knowledge of my previous operations to convince anyone from our side that you are me and remember if all else fails ramble, remember you're suffering from battle fatigue".

The Major was interrupted by a loud knock on the room door followed by an abrupt announcement, "Ten minutes to Ryton's transport sir". This prompted the Major into a hurried response, "No problem Thompson that'll be all". Syd immediately recognizing the voice of one of the other enlisted men tending the Officers.

As his footsteps could be heard disappearing down the corridor, the Major realized that he's spent perhaps too much time going over Syd's life rather than concentrating on getting across some key points of his.

"Ten minutes Syd not long left to get across 6 months or more of intense desert fighting and all that, that entailed, I'm going to have to be damned brief here and just out line key points and events, and hope they're enough.

Following 'Operation Biting' which did really put us on the map in a military sense, it was back to intense training and trying to establish as many trained airborne battalions as we could in readiness for a counter attack on which ever front would present itself. Sometimes it felt like we had to beg borrow and steal resources to get things rolling.

Competition was intense, there even being some dispute as to which force should have ultimate control of airborne troops, but with some luck and a lot of tenacity and under the command of Major General Browning, by spring 1942 we had raised three battalions, and you could say from that point on we were fully fledged and ready for war.

The first full scale military use of the airborne forces came with Operation Torch which was the allied invasion of North Africa so you could say Syd that the deserts of North Africa is where the Parachute Regiment first cut its teeth.

From a personal perspective, my first action in the campaign was on the 29th November with the 2nd parachute battalion in Operation Oudna' where our objective was to secure the airstrip and destroy any enemy aircraft stationed there; Poorly equipped and with very limited intelligence, or maps we were landed at an abandoned airfield close to Oudna, jumping from American Dakota aircraft piloted by crew with little or no experience in airborne operations, with the landing site having to be selected by sight from the air, from the lead aircraft. We suffered seven casualties in that first jump one being fatal. Despite this set back we pressed on to our objective that being the airfield at Oudna arriving there mid-morning on the 30th only to find that the airfield there had also been abandoned. Unfortunately, we were spotted and attacked by German tanks supported by Stuka dive bombers and although the attack was driven back, we sustained heavy casualties and by dusk it was decided to withdraw to the west to a more defendable position and take count of our situation. Besides this we were to learn on the morning of the 31st of November that the allied push from the west towards Tunis had been postponed and we now had no choice but to retreat west to try and get back to allied lines some 50 miles away. Now that the Germans were aware of our presence and position they soon dispatched an armored column to engage us and despite a planned counter attack in the form of an ambush of the column, before it could be properly executed, the Germans became aware of our intention and so it did not work out well. Outgunned and outnumbered we were soon suffering extensive casualties and were forced to withdraw to higher ground to lick our wounds. Then as luck would have it just as we thought we were done for, the German armored column was mistaken for us by their own aircraft and they were attacked with bombs and machine gun strafing causing extensive casualties and with the loss of several of their tanks.

We had now taken around 150 casualties and so were forced to leave our wounded behind guarded by a small number of men as we tried to make our way back to allied lines. With the German armor in hot pursuit we retreated to an Arab farm but were quickly surrounded and our retreat was cut off. Now Syd we were in trouble the remaining 200 or so of us holed up in a farm and surrounded by German armor and getting damned low on ammunition. It was now 2nd of December and it was decided even though practically suicidal, our only hope was to fight our way out and this we did. During the night, we attacked the weakest part of the German defenses and broke out and then believe it or not were rallied by Lieutenant Colonel John Frost's hunting horn bringing all the stragglers trailing behind and outside the farm together. We then marched for the town of Medjez el bab and finally joined up with American patrols on the 3rd of December having sustained casualties comprising 16 officers and 250 other ranks, this was our first defeat or perhaps that is a little harsh, let's say our first knock back and it was disheartening, but did serve to sharpen our resolve.

This was just the start of what was to become a bloody campaign Syd and a campaign against a determined, highly professional, and well-equipped enemy, you could say we had certainly met our match.

As the Tunisian campaign went on we seemed to play out a never-ending game of cat and mouse exchanging gains and losses on an almost daily basis".

Syd listening intently interrupted, "Ryton with me not having any experience of desert war, but I'd say my fair share of European battle fields, how does the battle differ, give me some well-known differences and similarities in case I get called on it".

"That's a damned good question Syd and one I'm going to have difficulty answering in such a short time, but here goes", and the Major rubbing his chin a little thought for a moment then began.

"The 'stench of death', remains the same Syd, that never changes, although the heat brings it on sooner but dries a corps more quickly. The death siren of a diving Stuka remains the same Syd, whether it be in North Africa or the Somme Valley, I'll hate that noise until the day I die, and the bombs they drop, they are the same and have the same devastating result. Tanks are tanks, artillery is artillery, war is war, and men are men, the only difference is the theater in which it is all played out Syd, it all comes down to the specific theater of war. The main difference in desert warfare, I'd say is cover or indeed the lack of it, it's a more raw form of fighting all more open you could say with men being driven to their absolute limits and beyond and the intense fury of that war exacerbated by; Heat, desert, sun, sand, thirst, hunger, fatigue, snakes that can kill you, spiders that can kill you, and scorpions oh those damned scorpions, they can kill you too, and that's just the beginning". The Major paused for a moment gathering his thoughts the pressed on "Of all the things out there in the desert that are different, the two that bothered me the most Syd was firstly the Camel Spiders, the ugliest things I've ever seen, giving a nasty bite, they can run faster than a man, are the size of a dinner plate, are not poisonous, but do give you serious respect for all things creepy crawly and reminds one to leave all things that crawl and dwell amongst the rocks well alone. Secondly and worse still for me though was the sand, the damned sand, not easy and too hot to walk on or in during the day, especially in the dunes, everything seems to be governed by it, and ultimately consumed by it, it's a constant battle, and one that's never won, it gets everywhere, and I mean everywhere Syd, in your eyes, in your ears, in the crack of your arse, even under your foreskin. So, Syd if anyone asks about desert war that's what you need to tell them, just reiterate what I've just said and they'll have a pretty good chance of believing you've been there".

"I'll remember that and remember it well" commented Syd, "but what of the rest of the Tunisian Campaign Ryton, any quick remarks or history I need to know?"

The Major again rubbed his chin "Six months of sheer bloody hell Syd, intense fighting as I've already mentioned, men on both sides being reduced to nothing more than brutal primeval fighting objects, but for those that survived men with a bond of common experience, and a bond that can never be broken. The campaign did see me awarded the DSO and given a field promotion to Major, for sure you need to know that, and command of a company in the second battalion of the parachute regiment. A rapid climb up the ranks, you could say that Syd, but one not won lightly. Our Battalion had started the campaign with 24 officers and 588 men, along the way we had 230 reinforcements, and by the end of the campaign were left with 14 officers and 346 men of various ranks. That's one hell of an attrition rate Syd one hell of an attrition rate indeed and every one of those men, the finest fighting troops and men of distinct honor, that's how we were referred to after the battle.

That just about sums everything up here Syd but one last question very quickly what would you say are the two most important things I should know as a member of a machine gun battery?" The Major asking this to lighten the mood just prior to his departure.

This time it was Syd's turn to ponder for a brief moment, "That's easy" commented Syd, "How do you stop a runaway gun, answer pull a bullet out of the belt, very important to know that and secondly, never ever let the barrel cooling tank run dry supposing it has to run on piss which indeed much of the time the guns were!" and with that Syd smiled a little but perhaps more in apprehension.

The Major chuckled a little at Syd's comments realizing that even in the depths and depravities of war a sense of humor must still preside.

"Right then all that remains is to say best of luck sir" Syd replying, "You too Ryton" and with that the Major now fully emplaced as Lance Corporal Sydney Ryton turned to the door and closing it behind him was gone with nothing but his fading footsteps echoing down the corridor. Syd sat there for some time as the stark reality of what he'd just taken on, hit home and hit home pretty damned hard and more so as he stood and went to the window and looking down on the courtyard could see the prisoner transport truck leaving through the guarded gate. "It all starts from here" thought Syd then suddenly there was a knock on the door, "Five minutes to Lunch sir" came the announcement from the other side of the door. Syd's reply almost instinctive. "Thank you Thompson I'll be down directly".

End of Part One.

23970536R00097

Printed in Great Britain
by Amazon